FULL CONTACT WRITING

*How to Win with Fearless Communication
in a "Show No Mercy" Workplace*

RG Gardner, Ph.D.

© 2025 by RG Gardner

All rights reserved. No part of this book may be reproduced or transmitted in any form or by any means, electronic or mechanical, including photocopying, recording, or by any information storage and retrieval system, without permission in writing from the copyright owner.

FCW Press

What others are saying about **Robert Gardner** and *Full Contact Writing*…

"Effective, concise writing is critical in today's markets. Robert Gardner shows how to simply get your message across and get the action and response you want. If you communicate, you need to read this book."

Senior Vice President
Computer Sciences Corporation (CSC)

"Today, more than ever, words matter. If you want your writing to stand out, then you'd better learn from the best, and there's no one better than Bob Gardner."

Senior Systems Engineer
Integrated Communication Solutions

"Lucid, clear, smart, helpful, and very powerful advice from a writing expert who knows what it takes to energize business communication (and did I mention entertaining?)..."

Quality Assurance Manager
United BioSource Corporation

"In business, professionalism and success come from the ability to communicate effectively. Bob Gardner's guide will give you the edge you need."

Entrepreneur
Small Business Owner

"Robert Gardner is an enthusiastic and dynamic writer. I've used his strategies to produce numerous winning grant proposals. The positive impact you'll get from Full Contact Writing will be huge."

Chief Neuroscientist
St. Jude Children's Research Hospital

"Bob Gardner has written an indispensable guide for writing to win in the digital era. He provides clear, on point, and extremely helpful advice on how to turn passable business writing into a powerful and persuasive tool for success."

Senior Principal Engineer
Lockheed Martin Corporation

"Two outs, bottom of the ninth. Thanks for coming through for us Bob. We knew we could count on you and your Full Contact Writing approach to make this proposal a winner!"

Capture Manager
General Electric Company
Government Services Division

"Fast-changing times in the business world call for a writing style that's tight, flexible, and adaptable. Think Full Contact Writing."

President and CEO
Training Educational Services
Non-profit Organization

To Victoria, for always believing in me.

"He was intrigued by the power of words. Not the literary words that filled the books in the library, but the sharp, staccato words...words that went for the jugular."

—*Robert Cormier,* I Am the Cheese—

CONTENTS

SINK OR SWIM 1

TIME TO GET PERSONAL 3

FULL CONTACT WRITING: WHERE EVERY WORD COUNTS 6
- WHAT IT IS 6
- WHAT IT LOOKS LIKE 7
- WHY IT MATTERS 9
- IS FULL CONTACT WRITING WHAT YOU NEED? 10
- THE PILLARS OF FULL CONTACT WRITING 11

THE A-C-E MODEL: YOUR DELIVERY PLATFORM 12

A-C-E STEP 1: AIM AT YOUR TARGET 14
- "SEE" WHAT I'M SAYING? 14
- HIJACK THEIR ATTENTION 16
- LET'S DIALOGUE 17
- DO I KNOW YOU? 17
- WHAT'S IN IT FOR ME? 19

A-C-E STEP 2: SET YOUR COURSE OF ACTION 22
- WRITING IS THE ART OF VALUE CREATION 22
- ALWAYS A SITUATION-BASED STRATEGY 23
- DON'T JUST COMMUNICATE—*MOTIVATE* 24
- WRITE FOR ACTION, NOT INFORMATION 26

A-C-E STEP 3: EXECUTE THE GAME PLAN 28
- FIVE DEADLY SINS: COMMON WRITING EXECUTION MISTAKES 29
  - *mistake #1: excessive hype* 29
  - *mistake #2: forgetting to sell* 30
  - *mistake #3: the "yadda yadda yadda" syndrome* 31
  - *mistake #4: "can you hear me now?"* 32
  - *mistake #5: show-stopping screw-ups* 33
  - *other (dis)honorable mentions* 34
- WORDS: LINKING STRATEGY TO RESULTS 37
  - *get the most from the fewest* 37
  - *understand the gist of jargon* 37
  - *you're judged by the words you choose* 40
  - *and know this: the sound of words matters* 40
  - *must do—starting now* 41
  - *buzzwords and misguided purists* 44

SENTENCES: LEADING THE CONVERSATION 46
   set the rhythm of the dance 46
   control the dialogue 47
   use strong directional cues 48
   another good control tactic 49
   addition by subtraction: keep sentences short 49
   build cadence into your sentences 50
   sentence imperatives: summing it up 52
PARAGRAPHS: HOLDING IT TOGETHER 53
   ask the right questions 53
   stir with imagery 54
   hook and hold 56
CARDINAL RULE: DO NOT PROJECT "INCOMPETENT" 58
BIG FINISH 59
YOUR NEXT STEP: JUMP IN AND SWIM! 61

WRITING IN ACTION: NOTES FROM THE PROVING GROUND 62
   ALWAYS WRITE TO WIN 63
   PROTECT YOUR REPUTATION 64
   SYSTEM FAILURE: NOT SO TRANSPARENT TO THE USER 66
   FORCING FUNCTION AND WRITING TO MOVE 68
   THE BEST WAY TO DRAIN POWER FROM YOUR WRITING PUNCH 69
   FIVE SAY-NOTHING PHRASES TO QUICKSAND NOW 71
   NUKE THESE OLD WRITING MYTHS 72
   YOU CAN'T SAY THAT AGAIN… 73
   "NETERATURE" AND YOU 74
   PRACTICE THE ART OF PERSUASION 75
      it's words that sell—everything 76
      more notes on persuasive language 77
      push benefits, not features 78
      the binds that tie 78
      when to use manipulative language 80
      a quick word about spin doctors and sound bites 81
   GOOD NEWS/BAD NEWS 81
      driving results: the good news/bad news letter 83
   LIFE, DEATH, AND THE PSYCHOLOGY OF EMAIL 85
      how to do email the right way 86
   GRAMMAR: THE ELEPHANT IN THE ROOM 89
      respect the rules—but don't bow to them 89
      not "correctness"—effectiveness 89
      essential vs. "fake" rules: know the difference 90
      when to ignore "proper English"(and when not to) 91

    abbreviations 91
    colloquialisms 92
    contractions 92
    em dashes 92
    imperatives 92
    a crash course on commas 92
    second person pronouns (briefly) 93
    bottled smoke: the good, the bad, and the very ugly 93
  ANATOMY OF A WINNING PARAGRAPH 95
  POWERPOINT: SOME FUNDAMENTAL TRUTHS 98
    a note from the field 98
    six more must-knows for Powerpoint success 99
  BUSINESS LETTERS DEMYSTIFIED 101
    how to write one 101
    a dumb letter 103
    job seekers: nail the cover letter! 105
  EMULATE SUCCESS 107
    the beat goes on: "borrow" what works 108
    four takeaways from Ernest Hemingway 108
    10 final hints on how to write 110
  FOR GOOD MEASURE: MORE TOOLS FOR WRITERS 111
    a few good blogs on business writing 112
    some great websites for help with grammar 112
    more websites on words (and how best to use them) 113

FOR YOUR ROAD AHEAD 114
  FIVE REMINDERS 114

ABOUT THE AUTHOR 115

INDEX 116

SINK OR SWIM

"The good news is, thanks to the Web, people are writing again. Email. Chats. Tweets. Web sites. Blogs. The bad news is, people are writing again."
—Anonymous—

Type. Spell check. Save. Send.

Another day, another writing chore. Another push to get the right words out of your head, up on the screen, and out to your world of waiting readers. It's part of your job, and you deal with it the best way you can. Business as usual, right?

Not exactly.

SPOILER ALERT: Whenever you write, there's a vast, unseen force working against you.

You may not give it much thought. But it's out there, and it's not your friend.

What is it? Let's call it **INFO GLUT**.

According to Google Executive and former CEO Eric Schmidt, every two days we create as much information as we did from the dawn of civilization up until the year 2003. That comes out to something like five exabytes of data.

It's an astounding observation—one with deep implications for all of us who work for a living. We're adding to this mind-boggling, global explosion every time we sit down to a keyboard.

It doesn't matter whether your communication is one-to-one (like emails, letters, resumes, IMs), one to several (proposals, marketing pitches, group emails), or one to potentially thousands (blogs, web copy). Every time you cut your words loose to sink or swim in this rising tide of *content*, you're hoping you've done enough to get the results you want.

Sorry to burst your bubble, but there's a better-than-even chance you haven't.

Thanks to this spreading data smog, writing in today's business world has morphed into a physical, *full-contact* sport. Now, your words compete for the hearts and minds of people who are themselves busy competing through their own communication. We're all struggling to navigate through the noise.

Sound like a tough sell? *It is.*

Yours is one of millions of voices, fighting to be heard in an ever-widening arena of players. It's a high-stakes game, folks. Winners get the glory. Losers go home.

It doesn't matter whether you're a "seasoned" professional or a 20-something who's just landed a first job. Your reputation is on the line every time you write.

You have skin in the game.

So what are you going to do about it? Continue to rely on what you think you know about writing? Keep telling yourself "If it's not broken, don't fix it?"

Sure, those are options. (After all, you may have been treading water up till now, and you're still floating, right?)

But there's a better way. My experience tells me there's a more immediate, proven approach to improving the odds your communication won't end up in some black hole—"out there." Ignored and forgotten.

After all, it's now warfare. When you write at work, you're always under siege. And you should be armed.

That's where **FULL CONTACT WRITING** comes in.

TIME TO GET PERSONAL

"A powerful agent is the right word. Whenever we come upon one of those intensely right words…the resulting effect is physical as well as spiritual, and electrically prompt."
—Mark Twain—

What if I told you it's likely you're peddling *dead words* on the job—words with little power, and even less value? Would it bother you if you discovered your writing is probably working against you, which is why you often can't get anything (or anyone) to work <u>for</u> you?

Both of these assertions are valid. (Don't shoot the messenger.) You've been neglecting the care and feeding of your writing and it's costing you—often in ways you're not even aware of, until it's too late.

Time to start thinking about the solution.

What fervent action can you take today, right now, to get your writing off of life support and *back in business?*

How about a model, a set of trench-tested strategies to kick-start your communication style and get people to sit up and take notice?

Interested?

OK. Here's what has to happen before anything else:

Your writing must get personal.

This means writing like you're looking somebody square in the eye, telling them, point blank, what you want them to do for you—and why they should. When you do that, your product captures the sound and characteristics of **speech acts**.

Speech acts are powerful because most of the actions that people engage in during the course of everyday life are carried out through conversation. That's why you should write like you speak. And learn to speak like you're writing. Logical, right?

But here's the deal: Most people speak and write without *intention*. They often simply say or write whatever comes to mind, with no strong sense of direction, or thought about outcome. The result? Unpredictable, at best.

But when you're communicating with purpose, your reader's impression of you takes on a new, exciting dimension.

That makes shaping reader perception your number one concern. Problem is, it's getting tougher to find ways to make this happen with any kind of reliability or consistency when we're bombarded with such a high volume of *mass*-produced words.

Which brings us to where we are now. In this **Age of Immediacy**, writing has turned into a "get there by the most direct route available" proposition. This means you need to find and follow less-traveled paths to adjust and advance. You don't have a choice. Those old rules of the road don't cut it anymore.

Well chosen (and well placed) words do work. And they sure as hell matter. They have force. They have energy. They can and will do things for you.

> **TRUE STORY:** *I once got the number 2 man at the (then) second largest US computer manufacturing company to do exactly what I wanted him to do...*
>
> *...I persuaded him to make an exception to his company policy and fix my dead PC for free, even though my warranty had expired. My letter drove this guy to direct action. And I saved hundreds of dollars. This was one of my earliest Full Contact Writing wins. Naturally, it fueled my appetite for more!*

Success like this hits home when you start looking at your writing as your *product*—something you manufacture and sell in *your* marketplace. Your words are the trusted elements of that product.

Learn it. Live it. Love it.

If I sound borderline fanatical about this, I am. Through trial and error in the broadest range of work situations, I've forged a healthy respect for the power dynamic that exists between a writer and reader. I've seen firsthand what happens when writing fails to do its job—the time wasted, dollars lost, and opportunities missed.

Working with words is a business—a serious business. And it's <u>my</u> business. Stretching the capacity, the influence, of the written word—exploring the high-voltage connection between language and action—has grown to be my passion. It would be great if it became <u>your</u> passion too.

Here's one more thing I learned. Scores of people in corporate America—up and down the food chain—have one thing in common: They want their writing to matter. They want their words to make a difference.

Like you, they're looking for:

>   Words that dance
>   Words that sing for their supper
>   Words that move somebody from here to *there*.

Interested in going all in with **FULL CONTACT WRITING**?

OK, then it's time to adjust your thinking…

Writing in the work world is a business transaction. That means every piece of writing you create has potential value.

It's got to bring you a solid return on your time investment. It has to *make something happen*.

ALWAYS.

FULL CONTACT WRITING: WHERE <u>EVERY</u> WORD COUNTS

> *"Get to the point! Blurt it out!*
> *Tell me plainly what's in it for me!"*
> —*Roy H. Williams,* The Wizard of Ads—

Challenging times demand firm, positive action. (And if there's one word to describe today's business world, it's "challenging.") We all know the imperatives handed down from on high. We hear about the constant challenge to stay competitive. To do things better, faster, cheaper. To do more with less.

When it comes to writing for *your* world of work, your main challenge has never changed: Find a way to connect with your time-and-attention-starved readers. Then persuade them to do something.

We're talking about your colleagues, management, and customers. **You need to convince these people that you're someone they want to do business with.** It's that simple.

"Doing business" means writing to help somebody else achieve one or more of these five basic outcomes:

>Save money
>Make money
>Solve a problem
>Sidestep failure
>Avoid pain.

WHAT IT IS

Full Contact Writing is a means to that end. It's a minimal, uncomplicated approach to business writing. An approach that's about mastering **action language**—knowing how and when to generate a message that cuts to the chase, takes hold, stirs, and *moves*.

Why the need? Because in our get-it-done-now, profit-and-loss world, <u>every</u> word must count! That's why the writing you wrestle with every day has got to carry the content of immediacy. It's no-holds-barred, and often *in your face*.

FULL CONTACT.
Get <u>in</u> with the message. Get <u>out</u> with results.

Great war cry, right? It sounds good. But how do you implement? What do you have to *do* to improve your odds of writing success?

Answer: You look for fresh, no-nonsense ways to move your words. You practice and perfect a cut, chiseled style of writing that calls to act, and **wins**.

WHAT IT LOOKS LIKE

> *"Chaos is a friend of mine."*
> *—Bob Dylan—*

Smart professionals find a way to thrive in an uncertain, fast-moving world. They know that with so much content that's just click on, click OUT, they're writing for readers who rely almost exclusively on a visual medium for their input.

The emphasis has shifted away from traditional, more formalized, subject+verb+predicate, linear information.

The **FULL CONTACT WRITING** focus:

- High-impact words and phrases
- Hard-hitting, quick-crunch sentences
- Fast reader retention

Readers pull words from their monitor, which means they're using the same part of their brain they use to watch TV. So lose the "hardcopy" mentality. People respond differently to pixels on a screen than they do ink on a page.

The **FULL CONTACT WRITING** focus:

- Easy reading formats (Wide lines across the screen slow readers down. Narrow lines speed them up.)

Technology never stops impacting the way your readers think. And <u>act</u>.

The **FULL CONTACT WRITING** focus:

- Writing that exploits a reader's ability (and desire) to make lightning-quick decisions
- Simple, easy-to-follow ideas
- Vertical stacking of phrases—giving readers a visual shape where less detail is lost

People are being reprogrammed to write and speak in shorter sentences. The brain is losing its ability to keep track of complex phrases and clauses.

The **FULL CONTACT WRITING** focus:

- Writing that's fast and on-point
- No run-on sentences
- Strategic use of fragments for emphasis and traction
- Similar topics grouped in easy-to-digest chunks

With these nonstop time and attention challenges, even if we want to read or write longer, more textured prose, we may not be able to.

The **FULL CONTACT WRITING** focus:

- More high-impact sentence clusters to carry your intentions more forcefully
- A plainer, less punctuated writing style with more line spaces; action verbs and no "filler"

WHY IT MATTERS

This one's easy. In a content-focused economy, so much is communicated by the written word. Even if you've got all the other skills, and not writing, you have a weakness.

So writing today requires a stand-out strategy of power, a model of "winning friends and influencing people."

> **When you're writing from a position of strength and confidence, you're keeping your world moving forward.**
>
> **You're making things happen.**

The implications are both exciting and challenging. This digitally driven work world forces changes in the form and function of your writing, the platform you use to deliver your words, and the final structure of your product...
...which in turn drives changes in how you use words, the way you construct sentences, and how you build paragraphs to carry those sentences.

Your success with Full Contact Writing will follow when you come to understand the full implications of these relationships. Then, your written product will reflect that understanding. Naturally and instinctively.

But you have to <u>want</u> it.

Good writing starts with desire.

> *"The successful search for excellence in today's turbulent times requires a continuing dissatisfaction with the status quo and a deeply held belief that we can do better, we can be better."*
>   —Tom Peters—

You *can* be a better writer.

Believe it.

IS FULL CONTACT WRITING WHAT <u>YOU</u> NEED?

Time for a quick reality check before we move ahead. Full Contact Writing may not be for everybody. Some people may be satisfied with their current writing style. Or they may be reluctant to take on a more aggressive, head-on commitment to make their writing anything other than what it already is. Here's a way to tell if the guidance you'll find in this book is for you.

You're a prime candidate for Full Contact Writing if one or more of the following applies to you:

- You don't see yourself as a "writer." But you want some tips, some just-in-time strategies, for connecting with your audience.

- You want to energize and flex your daily writing style for a broad range of readers, people with diverse wants and needs.

- You want a more reliable (and repeatable) delivery system for your business writing.

- You're looking for ways to make your passable writing more engaging—more impactful.

If you show up in any of these requirement categories, you're just looking to write better. I get that. The Full Contact Writing approach will put you on the right path—and keep you there.

> **FACT:** *You have good reason to be confident. Almost anyone can learn to write clearly and persuasively. There's no special background or training required. No matter how ineffective you think your writing is today, you can make it better.*

> Is it marketing? Sure.
> Street smart? You bet.
> Persuasive? **ALWAYS.**

THE PILLARS OF FULL CONTACT WRITING

Writing in business is demanding and urgent, with an outsized status and instant effect (benefit or disaster).

- Your reader forms an impression of you in *real time*. Success is black and white.

- Your writing must always be going somewhere, toward somebody else's discovery, feeling, *action*.

- The e-world responds to sound bites, fragments, images, and flickering impressions. Quick content access with fast payoff is the primary currency of our culture. The Full Contact Writer understands this reality—and embraces it.

- Whenever you write, you're in the *influence business*. That means that whatever you have to do to get into your reader's head (and stay there) is fair game.

- Your goal: *transformation*. You're seeking a "do this now" imperative with your language—one that carries your agenda to the proper level of force and importance with your audience.

You don't have to be a word magician to produce high-charged writing that succeeds. You just need to know how to move forward with a style that's tight, flexible, and responsive to change.

Good writing deserves respect. Bad writing doesn't.

That's the "what" of **FULL CONTACT WRITING**.

Now let's dig into the how.

THE A-C-E MODEL: YOUR DELIVERY PLATFORM

"Strategy without tactics is the slowest route to victory. Tactics without strategy is the noise before defeat."
—Sun Tzu—

When you team with engineers, programmers, and other technical types long enough, you learn to put a high value on building systems that work the way they're supposed to work. You learn to understand how specific changes to process inputs and controls can produce a desired outcome.

Most of the people I worked with in the IT world were strong on the technical side of things, but they often stumbled badly when it came to the writing part of their job. So, over time, they came to see me as "the word guy"—somebody who could help them *engineer* solutions to their writing requirements.

To say the least, it's been an eye-opening experience. Through paying attention (and making way more than my share of mistakes), I developed a brass-tacks operating model for 95% of the 24/7 business writing that came out of my work environment. I call it the **ACE** model.

In a nutshell, here's how the pieces fit together:

- **A** = <u>A</u>IM (Analyze your target/audience.)
- **C** = <u>C</u>OURSE OF ACTION (Define the outcome.)
- **E** = <u>E</u>XECUTE (Develop and deliver the message.)

Simple, manageable, and effective.

ACE was spawned from writing tactics that delivered success. It's a selected collection of proven techniques that linked writer to reader, transferred a shared ambition, and forced a desired result. And it's a playbook that's always evolving!

Why "ACE?"

- In the tennis world, an ACE is a blistering, unanswered serve.
- In the gaming world, an ACE is the highest card in the deck.
- In aviation, an ACE is a top-notch fighter pilot.

In <u>your</u> world of business, ACE is a tested set of guidelines—the core components of a **win system** for the writing you do on the job.

Now take a look at the main components of the model.

A-C-E STEP 1:
AIM AT YOUR TARGET

"If you want to persuade me, you must think my thoughts, feel my feelings, and speak my words."
—Cicero—

You've got to begin by knowing your target. I mean <u>really</u> knowing your target. This is the part of the words-in-the-workplace game many people pay the least attention to. Too often, they rush to the keyboard in "Ready, Fire, Aim" mode.

Big mistake.

Business writing should be 80% mental preparation and 20% word processing.

That means that audience awareness is the one aspect of the communication process you should be honing in on with laser-like precision—well before any fingers start moving.

"SEE" WHAT I'M SAYING?

If you can't mentally converse with the person you're writing to, picture him or her sitting directly in front of you, you will <u>not</u> be in control of the situation. And you <u>won't</u> connect.

Think of it this way: Your readers are often nothing more than *moving targets*, jumping from one brush fire to another, putting one hose down and picking up another. Their "normal" is no time, even less focus.

> *"In the 'Attention Economy,' anyone trying to connect with an audience must treat the user's time as the ultimate resource."*
> —Jakob Nielsen, Nielsen Norman Group—

Knowing time isn't on your side, your task is to get inside your reader's decision-making cycle—with writing that *takes charge.*

You do this by giving "face time" to your words.

"Who are you and why should I care?" Imagine a talking head putting this question to you every time you write. True, the tone may sound cold and impersonal, but there's your audience. When your message synchs with that person, you're on your way.

> **NOTE:** *An audience is anyone who will listen to you or read what you've written. The operative word here is "anyone." This is another area where writers frequently run into trouble.*

What's more, an audience can be a pin-point-specific person you think you know well, people you know less well, and, given the far-reaching and ubiquitous power of the Internet, those you've never spoken to or met.

Something else to keep in mind: Because the scarcest resource for many of us is time, you're always competing with a lot of other priorities. The reason your reader is ignoring you may have nothing to do with your message—and everything to do with a crisis on the home front or a brutal, looming deadline. The dynamics are often behind the scenes—and they're always shifting.

Just be aware that consumers of your words expect their attention to be captured and sustained. No way is it good enough to start out well only to finish poorly.

**You're writing to unlock the traffic jam
in a busy reader's head.**

HIJACK THEIR ATTENTION

Don't be misled. When it comes to getting a fix on the full range of your reader's shifting demands, there's a common perception that time is your most valuable resource. It's not. We all have the same 24 hours in a day. When it comes to influencing and persuading others, your most coveted objective is securing and keeping someone else's ***attention***.

Think about it…

Have you ever seen one of those off-beat TV commercials where you have no idea what's being advertised until the end of the segment, when you're finally able to piece together the details, and lock into the sales pitch? That company just spent thousands of dollars (millions during the Super Bowl) on techniques to snag and hold your…***attention***. Right up to that last "ah HA!" moment.

When you have participants in a training class (or even in a one-on-one "teaching moment"), you have their time (they're typically required to be there). But if you want to have any real impact, you must own their ***attention***.

This means that to communicate with consistent effectiveness, you need to understand that attention <u>scarcity</u> is a given. Once that's crystal clear to you, you'll be writing to 1) align with the priorities people do have, or 2) become a solution to your reader's constraints.

> **RELATED FACTOID:** *Since 2000, the average human attention span has dropped to about 8 seconds. The attention span of a goldfish is 9 seconds. You heard that right—the attention span of an average person is now shorter than that of a goldfish. Talk about a huge challenge for a writer at work!*

As if that isn't enough, remember that, as your words pop up on somebody's screen, you don't have the luxury of being there to see what's working or what isn't. You can't see what's confusing or clear, what's accepted, rejected, or (worst of all) ignored.

LET'S DIALOGUE

Let's button down the preliminaries. These are the key criteria for producing a successful written message:

- It has to be an *invitation to dialogue*, not just your monologue. If your readers can't see themselves in the ambition of your message, it won't be shared. So don't create it in a vacuum. Take the necessary upfront time to understand the full dimensions of the transaction.
- It's got to be *compelling*. Even inspiring. It should be a statement of aspirations, rather than a dour warning of what someone's fate will be if they don't go along with you. Always pursue excellence rather than avoid failure.
- It must be in everyone's *line of sight*. You can't hit a target you can't see. Communicate the ambition and importance of your message in writing that builds a clear and inviting mental image.
- It must leave your reader resolved to *do something*.

Stash these away for safe keeping. They're the secrets to *holding* your reader's attention (after you pull off the hijacking).

DO I KNOW YOU?

This business of audience analysis can be a little tricky. That's because the body of readers you're addressing in any given writing engagement can be either simple or complex. A simple audience consists of your *primary target* and no one else. This primary target can be either a single person or a small group.

A *secondary audience*, on the other hand, consists of those who may also read what you've written, although they were not the original, or even the most important targets.

If you're writing to an audience of primary and secondary targets, you're dealing with a *complex* group of consumers.

> **ERGO:** *A good audience assessment must line up with the characteristics of <u>both</u> the primary and the secondary audiences.*

The two can sometimes vary greatly, so your task is to come up with a strategy that anticipates, targets, and ultimately wins over both.

Take this everyday example from *XYZ Corporation*:

> You're the manager of a 15-person department. You're writing to let your people know that as of a certain date you want them to fill out their expense reports, vacation schedules, and timesheets online, using the company's newly installed intranet.
>
> You're offering them two ways to learn this new procedure:
>
> - Complete a self-paced online training module for the software application you're using.
> - Sign up for a half-day tutorial class.
>
> In addition to the members of your department, you're copying your director of technical operations, the director of human resources, and the director of training. In this situation, you're dealing with a *layered target segment*.
>
> It breaks down like this...
>
> Your 15 employees are your primary audience. The technical operations director, HR director, and training director are your secondary audience.
>
> Your challenge is to connect with *both* of these layers. Make sure you're including everybody in this engagement.
>
> I would <u>not</u> advise going with this approach...
>
> *All –*
>
> *Employees are required to be trained in a new timekeeping software application we are rolling out at XYZ. You have two options for completing this mandatory training...*

...Instead, go with something like this...

All –

> *We're introducing a new, more efficient way of timekeeping here at XYZ. This change will make everyone's life easier, and we need your support and cooperation to ensure project success. Training is the key to making all of this happen, so we're offering all employees two ways to come up to speed on the new process....*

What do you think? Are there differences between the two groups of people you're talking to here? Absolutely. If you neglect either one of these segments by failing to define the boundaries of their wants and needs—their *hot buttons*—your writing will short circuit. (And so will your reputation as a manager who knows how to communicate objectives and win consensus.)

Without a doubt, assessing your audience can be a slippery slope. But it's the most important pre-planning part of the writing process. Don't sabotage your chances for success by cutting corners here.

WHAT'S IN IT FOR ME?

When you're out to sell people on doing anything, their response will be based on two internal questions—questions they process instantly. The first question is: "What's in it for me (WIIFM)?" In other words, "Is this something that holds *value* for me?"

If you get a "no" to this first question, it's no go. You will not be influencing that individual.

If you get a "yes" to the first question (in other words, they perceive there *is* something in it for them), the second question becomes: "Can I do this?" ("Am I capable?")

If you get a "no" to this question, once again, *zero influence*.

But, when you get a "yes" to both of these questions, you've opened a door. That person may now let you in, providing what you have to offer continues to hold perceived value.

So the lesson here is dead simple: First, get their **attention**. (Starting to see a pattern here?) Second, everything you communicate must be:

- Delivered in the context of what's in it for them.
- Fast, uncomplicated, and easy to follow.

As writers we have to navigate through situations like this all the time.

Careful, upfront reader analysis will help you set the proper tone and style for your message. Answering these basic questions is the best way to get started:

- Who is the primary audience? Do I have a secondary audience? If so, who is it? What do I know about them?
- What background knowledge and experiences do these people have regarding this communication?
- What's my relationship to the primary and secondary members of the audience? Am I a subordinate, supervisor, or equal colleague?
- What do I want my audience to do with my words? In short, how do I *define success* in this writing engagement? (You have to name it.)

Yes, your goal is to invade your reader's space. But it goes well beyond that. Once you have that space, you must *occupy* it.

A lousy start….

Dear Councilman Jones,
I am writing with the hope that you can assist me…

A <u>better</u> way…

> *Dear Councilman Jones,*
> *My vote helped get you re-elected. Now I need your help to fix a problem I'm facing…*

Remember your goal: **Engagement**. **Shared ambition**.

I'll bring it down to ground level. When it comes to gauging the impact your writing's having on your audience, your mantra should always be…

> *"Look at the results. There's truth in the results."*

And don't worry. If you keep to these fundamentals, you'll get to the point where audience analysis will be a process that's happening with you automatically.

> **TIP:** *Read Strunk and White's* The Elements of Style.

I know, I know. Practically every author who's ever written anything about writing will reference this book. And for good reason. It's valuable—for its clear, concise treatment of grammar and usage, and its constant focus on the importance of audience awareness.

> *"Chance favors the prepared."*
> —*Louis Pasteur*—

A-C-E STEP 2:
SET YOUR COURSE OF ACTION

*"If I had six hours to cut down a tree,
I'd spend four hours sharpening the axe."*
—Abraham Lincoln—

Strictly speaking, we don't "write" anymore. We create and manage <u>content</u>. It's the new integration of what you say and how you say it. And as you might guess, the demand has never been greater for actionable words.

Content is king.

All of this means that content is now, for various reasons, viewed or "purchased" as a commodity. When you write, you're producing a commodity for <u>purchase</u>. (In this context, there's a broad range of definitions for "purchase"—all of them are transaction-based: *accept, act upon, pass forward, approve, agree to,* etc.)

So it follows that different consumers require different content marketing strategies. Keep the following guidelines in mind when you're setting a course of action for your written communication.

WRITING IS THE ART OF VALUE CREATION

Never let your reader walk (or click) away. What's your *immediate* value proposition—and how will you seek reader buy-in? Once you define that, how are you going to *close the deal?*

Start by asking yourself two questions:

What do I need to do with my words?
How will I do it?

The late, great movie director Stanley Kubrick once said that "filmmaking is an exercise in problem solving." For him, the act of making a motion picture included paying close attention to the distribution and marketing of the movie, as well as its production. So he devoted more time and effort to managing the release of his films than any other director. He loved the problem-solving.

The same goes for your writing. Project planners call it the "problem space." It's the range of problems your reader's dealing with. What are you going to do to solve them—and how will you do it in a way that wins for <u>you</u> as well?

Reminds me of an interview I once had with a business executive who was building his marketing team at a start-up telecommunications company. In retrospect, I'd characterize the experience as a "character builder." As I sat there getting grilled and skewered, my glance kept landing on the oversized poster hanging on the wall just behind this guy's desk.

There was something about those big white letters against that stark, black background:

> "If you have anything important to say,
> *say it in the next five minutes*."

LESSON LEARNED: *Keep it short. Keep it simple. And keep it relevant.*

ALWAYS A SITUATION-BASED STRATEGY

Count on it. There will always be workplace scenarios where the strength of your writing is all you have. And that's OK.

1. Stay in charge of the situation.
2. Get that clear picture of what you want your words to do for you in that particular set of circumstances.
3. Then take a step back and think: "What message plays best for this engagement?"
4. Next, before you do any writing at all, pinpoint the *single idea* you want to get across. Write it down in one sentence

on a note pad. This is a <u>one-line</u> description of your objective.

I want to set up a meeting with Ken to explain my new product idea.

Buying this new software package will save our department thousands of dollars.

Use this quick descriptor as your controlling idea. It'll keep you focused and on target. Everything should then build logically and forcefully from this one sentence.

Finally, you're ready to design word constructions that reach out and command a response to the specific business requirement. *Design* your solution in a way that fits the task—that works to win.

> *"Most people make the mistake of thinking design is what it looks like. That's not what we think design is. It's not just what it looks like and feels like. Design is how it works."*
> —Steve Jobs—

DON'T JUST COMMUNICATE—*MOTIVATE*

I'm always amazed at the number of people who seem content with just nudging their words from point A to point B. It's like they've convinced themselves that by simply scraping up a message they think will meet the needs of their audience, they're done with the prep work. In their mind, they've properly assembled and transmitted the content that needed to be conveyed. Piece of cake. Mission accomplished.

C'mon.

Communicating in this context is <u>never</u> good enough. To nail down a desired outcome with your reader, you'd better bridge the gap between strictly communicating and *motivating*.

Consider this "less than effective" example from the training page on a defense contractor's website…

> *Introduction to Contractors Authorized to Accompany the Force (CAAF)*
>
> *An introductory course that addresses how the DoD type classifies contractors, while examining broad roles and responsibilities of both government and contractor personnel for successful employee deployment to support U.S. armed forces abroad with a focus on the guidance provided in the DFARs and various Department of Defense Instructions.*

…Yes, this writing does communicate. But does it *motivate?* Not so much. It comes off like a dry, one-way description of a training course. Nothing more, nothing less.

Now think about a way to make it better, more *engaging*. Here's a more inviting approach:

> *Department of Defense Instruction DoDI 3020.41 is a vital, must-know source of policy, procedures, and mandates concerning DoD contractor personnel authorized to accompany the U.S. Armed Forces (CAAF).*
>
> *This timely foundational course presents the core knowledge contractors want and use every day. In this training, you'll find everything you need to fully comply with the DoD's CAAF requirements.*
>
> *With special attention paid to the guidance provided in the DFARs and various Department of Defense Instructions, the course addresses how the DoD type classifies contractors, and pays special attention to the broad roles and responsibilities of both government and contractor personnel in successfully deploying employees to support U.S. Armed Forces abroad.*
>
> *If you're new to the world of CAAF—or you just want a refresher class to stay current with ever-shifting mandates—you need this course.*
>
> *Click <u>here</u> to sign up now!*

Shape the form and function of your message. **Tell** your reader what you want. And then **move** them to give it to you.

WRITE FOR ACTION, NOT INFORMATION

Etch this in concrete: Your goal should always be **action**, not education, or information. Focus on getting your reader to do something, and not to "think" something.

At first, this might come across as a careless, almost irresponsible attitude, but if you look at it a little closer, it makes sense.

> **FOR EXAMPLE:** *Do you know it's a good thing to get plenty of exercise? Do you know you shouldn't run up credit card debt? Do you know it's important to get a good night's sleep? Sure you do. Lack of knowledge isn't the root cause of why you don't follow through on this advice 100% of the time. Hence: Giving people more information doesn't lead to a solution.*

The primary job of Full Contact Writing isn't to convey knowledge. It's to **connect** and **provoke to act**.

Instead of starting with information to communicate, start with the obstacles, the stuff that's getting in the way of reader action. Speak to that and solve for that.

> **TIP:** *Always make it easier to achieve your writing objective by thinking through the barriers your audience might have for making a change.*

An ad I saw in a local newspaper illustrates my point. It was placed there by a high-speed Internet Service Provider. The picture shows a brand-new college graduate, striding triumphantly in cap and gown, carrying his freshly minted diploma. He's walking with his proud parents.

Beneath this visual is the message:

The faster the Internet,
The quicker the job search,
The sooner the student loans get paid.

No detailed description of the service features. No comparisons with other carriers. No price incentives. Just a bare knuckles message that speaks to a common problem shared by a precisely defined audience.

The parts snap together as neatly as an IKEA bookcase.

A-C-E STEP 3:
EXECUTE THE GAME PLAN

"Watch the turtle.
He only moves forward
by sticking his neck out."
—*Lou Gerstner, former CEO at IBM*—

The web has all but killed the great idea that you can have stand-alone writing products—communication only you and a carefully specified set of readers might see and care about. Now, with the Internet, everything is tangled in with everything else.

We're all connected—networked with our virtual neighbors in a vast global village. It's a wonder we don't feel like we're playing three-dimensional chess in a dark room every time we touch a keyboard.

Meanwhile, in the midst of all this intricate connectivity, one glaring fact remains: There are just too many different ways our writing can fail.

Maybe this explains why we're frozen, like the proverbial deer in the high beams, when it comes to writing boldly. We're hesitant to try new ways to make our writing succeed. That's tragic, because when we back away from the challenge, we end up missing the payoff that comes from finding those less-beaten paths to connection and success.

It's like going to a nightclub at 6:00 pm when all the fun doesn't start until midnight.

> **THE TAKEAWAY:** *Don't shy away from trying new ways to engage your audience, widen your influence, and bolster your reputation (your brand).*

Just be careful as you forge ahead. There are always landmines to avoid.

FIVE DEADLY SINS:
COMMON WRITING EXECUTION MISTAKES

Want a quick list of the things your readers hate the most? Here you go. Do yourself (and your consumers) a huge favor—don't be a perpetrator.

MISTAKE #1: EXCESSIVE HYPE

The word *hype* is an abbreviation of *hyperbole*, which means exaggeration or overstatement. Of course, the first job of your writing is to market—a product, a service, an objective, you. So it's often tempting to trot out nothing but superlatives, like *best, most, perfect*, or *greatest*.

> The *greatest* benefit we offer our customers is the *best, most efficient* hardware solution—one that will save them an *awesome* amount of time with system reconfigurations and upgrades.

> Rebecca delivered the *perfect* response to the customer's *most difficult* questions about the scope of our services. As a result of her *tremendous* level of enthusiasm and her *fantastic* preparation, she's positioned us to be the *absolute best* in our market space.

Problem is, readers have come to view this hype with skepticism. That's because they're flooded with it all the time. It's in ads, commercials, everywhere words are peddled.

> **CAUTION:** *Overuse of superlatives can work against you, eroding the force and quality of your message. Not good.*

Avoid this pitfall by using fewer, more precise **power words**—and giving them the room they need to do their job.

- Replace multiple adjectives or adverbs with just one that's more evocative or concise.

- Worst case, limit yourself to a maximum of two adjectives or adverbs you attach to any particular noun or verb.

- Try to find a more precise noun or verb that will eliminate the need for a modifier altogether.

- Use bullets to break up your points. Modifiers are easier to swallow when you dole them out in smaller portions.

MISTAKE #2: FORGETTING TO SELL

In contrast to ads or brochures that try too hard to sell, there's plenty of writing in the workplace that seems to ignore selling altogether. Most of the time, this happens when the writer uses empty phrases instead of a *selling point*.

You know it when you see it. There's usually a tired, wasted, lead-in, like this:

> *The following is a list of the product's benefits:*

OK, so your reader knows exactly what to expect from the content that follows. But who cares? It's hardly a bank vault move as an opener. Where's the call to action? Why waste a good opportunity to make another selling point?

The fix isn't hard. **Assert yourself!**

> This product will improve our efficiency in so many ways. It will *<benefit 1>*. And it will *<benefit 2>*. On top of all that, it will *<benefit 3>*…etc.

Always look at your written product with this fundamental question in mind:

> *"Am I taking full advantage of every opportunity to sell this audience on my product, my service, my agenda?"*

MISTAKE #3: THE "YADDA YADDA YADDA" SYNDROME

It's sure no secret. We're up to our eyeballs in anemic, lofty-sounding words and phrases. *Robust, integrated, objected-oriented technology, paradigm* – words like these swarm over all areas of business. Some terms have even managed to slip past the bouncer at the door and make their way into common usage. Others have a much shorter life span.

Look at this excerpt from an article in a web developer's trade publication. The writer was (I think) trying to motivate website owners to look for new ways to develop "quality" site content:

> *"After you create a content strategy, begin to implement and execute it through content acquisition and architecture. License or develop content to fill the holes you identified. Improve the return on investment of your current content through better data design or improved licensing agreements. Find ways to better leverage internal content assets.*
>
> *From improved plans for logically 'slicing' content for different demographics, to choosing new content partners for better overall value, content acquisition should ultimately allow you to mold your site into a better product and possibly create new revenue streams."*

If you're the one looking for better ways to drive people to your website, will this advice help ease your pain?

Maybe, but I doubt it. Open with a more inclusive style:

> *Once you've come up with the best strategy for moving your product or service content to market, look for the most effective platform to make it happen. If you still have gaps in your content, think about ways to close them through licensing or further internal development...*

Talk with your readers in words they understand. But when you do, don't come off sounding so "friendly" that you look like somebody who wants a hug. Assume you're not gonna get it.

One more thing: Cut out the rah, rah, rah stuff, already.

> *All –*
>
> *I wanted to take a moment to recognize the Top Performers for the month! Congratulations to our winners! Keep up the great work! Everyone is doing an unbelievable job! Thanks for everything you do each day in support of the program!*

Save the bang for when it counts. Don't overdo the exclamation marks—and the overdone enthusiasm.

A better way:

> *All –*
>
> *Another month, another great contribution from the team. Special shout-out to our top performers—Jeff Bannister, Sarah Riley, and Will Jenkins—for going above and beyond to exceed project goals. Thanks to everyone for the work you're doing to ensure our ongoing success.*

MISTAKE #4: "CAN YOU HEAR ME NOW?"

The second your reader is forced to fumble around to find the point of your message, you're done. Your communication has slipped into signal attenuation, and you're the one left standing without a chair.

Here's an example of what I mean:

> You're trying to sell your boss on a specific high-resolution computer monitor you need for more impressive graphics design work. You decide to send him a quick note to plant the seed, and you think it would be a nice touch to start with this quote from a magazine ad you saw for the model you want:
>
> *A Klee it's not. But who needs big dots?*

Cute. With a little luck, your boss might know Paul Klee is an early twentieth-century painter. On the flip side, there's also a fair chance he won't know Klee from Klum. In other words, luck can't be part of your writing plan. Don't try to be cute.

A more concrete, unfiltered first sentence might be:

I found a monitor that's equal to the uncompromising level of quality and performance you expect from me.

Here, you're setting up a win-win opportunity for everybody—right out of the gate. Your boss gets a better work product from you, and you get the monitor you want.

"Creating something that sounds brilliant, playfully using connotations and derivations back to Latin and Greek, could gain points among your intellectual peers, but it creates unnecessary complexity, and sets you up for an ugly sell. Bypass your need to impress for your need to get things done."
   —Stafford Green, the Coca-Cola Company—

MISTAKE #5: SHOW-STOPPING SCREW-UPS

Proofread everything you send out at least twice. Typos, stupid grammar mistakes, blatantly incorrect punctuation, and missing words will cripple your credibility.

Don't rely on the grammar check feature in MS Word. It won't, for example, flag every instance of passive voice, and its recommended solutions for other "problems" it picks up aren't always good choices.

> **REMEMBER:** *Everything you write goes to perception. Why give anybody a chance to use you as a punch line because your work screams out "careless?"*

You'll stay on safe turf if you remember that writing success, like anything else, hinges on mastering the *mechanics*. It's about managing and respecting the linkage between words, word choice, sentences, sentence structure, and paragraphs.

OTHER (DIS)HONORABLE MENTIONS

Excessive Use of Passive Voice

Which sentence is more powerful?

> *Configuration management is a subject that's little known by most stakeholders.*

> *Most stakeholders don't know a thing about configuration management.*

If you chose the second sentence, well done. You know that framing your words in the active voice produces a more forward-moving, vigorous message.

> **WRITE THIS DOWN:** Every time you feel compelled to use the word "is" or another form of the verb "be" as the main verb in your sentence, get up and take a walk until that feeling passes. (While you're walking, come up with another word that will do a better job.)

> For example, instead of writing:

> *"Janette was saying she felt nervous when she said..."*

> Try: *"Janette acknowledged her nervousness when she said..."*

Sentences that Drone on Forever

> *For all intents and purposes, the reason our product pitch to the customer failed to connect was due to the fact that they stopped listening five minutes after Jim's weak opening remarks. (**32** words)*

> *Jim started the presentation with a weak opening, so the pitch died a quick death. (**15** words)*

Full Contact Writing

Forced Use of Complex Words Instead of Simple Ones

How to screw it up:

> *Jim –*
>
> *We should pursue this product as a possibility for the lab. Reliability, availability, and maintainability are ensured by the product's built-in reliability, symmetric multiprocessor architecture with comprehensive redundancy options for no single point of failure, on-line hot swap and dynamic reconfiguration capabilities, and an easily maintainable hardware and software design.*

Yawn. That was a short-cut to nowhere. You can just sense the room emptying.

More to the point, what **behavior change** can the writer expect to achieve from this communication? Granted, this sounds like it's written from one technical person to another, but is the sender gaining converts?

Here's a way to get off the ropes and back into the middle of the ring:

> *Jim –*
>
> *This product delivers considerable upside for our lab that we can't ignore:*
>
> - *It boasts a symmetrical multiprocessor architecture that's proven reliable, available, and maintainable.*
> - *It offers comprehensive backup options. No bottlenecks. No single point of failure.*
> - *We can exchange components and reconfigure the unit while it's online. No down time.*
>
> *We have good reason to be excited about the possibilities here. I'll check your schedule and set up a meeting to close on this.*

OK. That's a broad-brush of what *not* to do with your writing. All common mistakes—all fixable.

Now I'll show you how the building blocks of *Full Contact Writing* should fit together to give you the product you're looking for.

WORDS: LINKING STRATEGY TO RESULTS

"Words...They're innocent, neutral, precise, standing for this, describing that, meaning the other, so if you look after them you can build bridges across incomprehension and chaos. But when they get their corners knocked off, they're no good anymore. I don't think writers are sacred, but words are. They deserve respect. If you get the right ones in the right order, you can nudge the world a little..."
—Tom Stoppard—

Any time you write, your words are your wealth.

And the work products you trust to *carry* those words are as indispensable as a top-dollar money manager. After all, you care about the value of your investment portfolio. Why aren't you giving the same attention to capturing a greater return from your writing?

Read on for some essential rules of **word management**.

GET THE MOST FROM THE FEWEST

Say everything you need to say in as few words as necessary. It's your big, important message put as briefly as possible.

Your goal: *Maximum* clarity. *Minimum* words.

If you can cut a word and still keep the sentence's core meaning, the sentence is wordy.

UNDERSTAND THE GIST OF JARGON

Jargon happens when you rely on technical or area-specific terminology to get your point across. You're using a limited vocabulary to speak to a small circle of people.

It's not always a bad thing. For example, jargon may come into play when you're talking about some particular benefit of a product, procedure, or the value of some new technology on your company's bottom line.

The test for whether or not to use jargon is easy. Ask yourself if most of your targeted readers will understand what you're

Full Contact Writing

saying when you drop some choice bits of it into your writing. If yes, move forward. If no, either use plain-spoken words, or take the time to further explain what you just told them.

Here's a short list of examples. Phrases like these are capturing significant air time in business today:

Land and expand - Selling a small, upfront solution to a client and then, after the sale, expanding on that solution within the client's environment

*The ACME team's plan is to **land** their application in IBM's stateside manufacturing locations **and** then **expand** future product lines to a broader range of functional segments within Big Blue's global organization.*

Evergreen thinking - A visionary idea that may not always have a practical application

*Frank opened the meeting by telling everyone that it would be a brainstorming session, where all possible outcomes would be considered. **Evergreen thinking** was not optional—it was encouraged.*

The 40,000-foot view - An overview of a job or a project

*After sharing **the 40,000-foot view** of the planned site relocation project, their CEO jumped into the minute details.*

Drink our own champagne - Using the same product you sell to your customers. (Champagne is almost a universal indicator of a good product.)

*Our sales team has so much confidence in the quality of our storage devices, we're **drinking our own champagne** and deploying the units in our offsite locations.*

Boil the ocean - To attempt to do something that's impossible

*Steve's going down a dangerous path with this proposal. He's **boiling the ocean** with the scope of his promised solutions.*

Full Contact Writing

Grab the low hanging fruit - Choose the simplest option or avenue to accomplish a task

The new process improvement project we're kicking off with the customer next week will give us an opportunity to identify the least time-consuming solutions first. ***Grabbing this low-hanging fruit*** *will demonstrate our expertise and win us new business.*

Keep a list of the buzz-worthy terms currently moving through your industry or work culture. Check out these additional examples from my world of IT business, sales, and marketing:

> *Best of Breed*
> *Break through the clutter*
> *Brick-and-mortar*
> *Calibrate expectations*
> *Client-centric*
> *Gold standard service*
> *Deep dive*
> *Event horizon*
> *Eyeballs on the issue*
> *Fulfillment issues*
> *Hyperlocal*
> *Make it pop*
> *Mindshare*
> *Operational transparency*
> *Management visibility*
> *Engrained in our DNA*
> *Touch point*

You'll hear phrases like these more and more in the corporate world. Every business has its own jargon.

Push it when it's hot. Drop it when it's not.

YOU'RE JUDGED BY THE WORDS YOU CHOOSE

Whether or not you made the right word choice is something only your audience can decide. Make errors (*lose/loose*), (*their/they're/there*), (*your/you're*), (*its/it's*), and they'll see you as a writer wannabe. Write by relying on big words, excessive jargon, and Machiavellian prose, and they'll perceive you as sticking your elitist nose in the air.

The result is always the same: **Disconnect**.

Choose words that reach out and invite, instead of push back—words that sound right to the ear and carry a kind of rhythm. You'll always know them when you hear them. Keep a notebook.

> **ANOTHER TIP:** Take every opportunity to swap dull words for "sticky" ones: Go to *Thesaurus.com* and plug in your boring words to find better synonyms.

Remember: Write with confidence, not with arrogance. And never be afraid to take a (calculated) risk.

AND KNOW THIS:
THE <u>SOUND</u> OF WORDS MATTERS

It's all about how words *sound* when they're used with other words. Words play off each other. When they're used in specific combinations, they form rhythm. So, whenever the situation dictates, go with words that work well together, like *red wine and steak,* or *a cold Corona and a hot beach*.

The way you test the rhythm of your word choice is to **read your writing aloud**. Do that and you'll find the flow—or, more importantly, what's *stopping* the flow, so you can fix it. You'll <u>hear</u> how the words interact.

MUST DO—STARTING NOW

Use Power Words

Grab your reader by the collar. Then, hold that grip with a hammerlock as your power words resonate and stir. Power words are lively, specific, and concrete; they're **active verbs, descriptive nouns,** and **vivid modifiers.**

Choose Specific Nouns

Use the most specific nouns you can find for the subject of your sentence. When it comes to persuading and motivating, words like *discovery, easy, guarantee, health, love, money, new, proven, results, safety, save,* and *you* have been recognized by psychologists as having a high impact on an audience. There are plenty more where these came from.

Google and find out.

Go with Pointed Verbs

A sentence can offer a moment of quiet, it can pulsate with energy, or it can just lie there, like a dead fish. What makes the difference? The verb.

Power verbs are your **spark plugs**. They deserve the love.

Words often used as nouns (*balloon, mushroom, flood, blast, swamp, gorge*) make the best power verbs.

And lively, descriptive terms like *boost, swell, snowball, accelerate, bloat, fatten, deepen, heighten, drown, flush, overwhelm, gush, swarm, overrun, crush, mob, explode, burst, erupt, shatter, rain, blow the lid off, maxed out, bursting at the seam, jack up, spike, merge,* and *squeeze out* will lead the charge and give your communication the punch and energy it needs to carry the day.

> *Treat. Teach. Build. Serve.*
> *Pfizer's formula to improve global health.*
> *—(newspaper ad)*

> *Save money.*
> *Live better.*
> *—Wal-Mart*

As best-selling author Stephen King once noted, "*The road to hell is paved with adverbs.*" Going with pointed, power verbs lets you eliminate adverbs, which all too often are just propping up a limp verb anyway.

> *speaks softly ---> whispers*
> *eats hungrily ---> devours*

Stay in the present tense, active voice, and imperative—using **pointed verbs**.

> *"Ask, and it shall be given you. Seek and ye shall find. Knock and it shall be opened unto you."*
> *—Matthew 7:7—*

Also, be sure to eliminate adverbs and prepositions that mindlessly repeat the sense of the verb, like *circle around*, *merge together*, *exact same thing*, or *mentally recall*.

Cut to the Chase

> "When you're drowning you don't think, 'I would be incredibly pleased if someone would notice I'm drowning and come and rescue me.' You just scream."
> *—John Lennon—*

Never come off sounding pompous, snobbish, or long-winded.

So get rid of this kind of stuff from your lexicon:

> *accordingly*
> *concerning*
> *due to the fact that*
> *for the purpose of*
> *nonetheless*
> *supplementary*
> *with regard to*

They're hardly examples of the "*don't-make-me-come-over-there*" attitude you want to project. The more of these zombies you can find and neutralize, the crisper, more focused your writing style becomes—and the more air time your words will command in the marketplace.

> *"Avoid using the word 'very' because it's lazy. A man is not 'very tired,' he is 'exhausted.' Don't use 'very sad,' use 'morose.' Language was invented for one reason, boys—to woo women—and, in that endeavor, laziness will not do."*
> —*Robin Williams* —
> *(from the film* Dead Poets Society*)*

And for crying out loud, don't beat around the bush.

Lose the expressions that soften your message in ANY way. *Decidedly, arguably, sort of, kind of, pretty much, in a sense* are useless to you. When these qualifiers slip into your writing you come off sounding like a shifty salesman. They blunt your momentum, strain your credibility, and prevent you from building any emotional connection with your reader. Even worse, they make you sound <u>doubtful</u> about what you're selling.

The result? Nobody's cashing in.

> *"It rarely adds anything to say, 'In my opinion'—not even modesty. Naturally a sentence is only your opinion; and you are not the Pope."*
> —*Paul Goodman*—

BUZZWORDS AND MISGUIDED PURISTS

I've touched on this already, but I'll add these final thoughts. I get a kick out of linguistic "purists" who wage their personal battles against the use of jargon. It's like that classic image of Don Quixote fighting the windmill.

Look, if your reader is accustomed to using and hearing buzzwords, slang, and jargon, you need to understand that—and tailor your strategy accordingly.

For example, marketers like to talk about exploiting customer "*pain points*." Proposal teams often refer to the need for "*forward-looking solutions*" when they're coming up with win themes. Business developers sell services designed to do the "*heavy lifting*" for a prospective client.

Understand the semantic currency of your audience, and spend it wisely.

If you come across like you're talking to some grumpy granny who only wants to talk in "plain English" (whatever that means today), and your reader is a buzzword advocate, you're almost certain to miss any win opportunity.

MORE TO THINK ABOUT...

Our conversational language is turning words that once carried a negative connotation into a kind of edgy slang, with strong, positive meaning. TV sports commentators and talk radio hosts have a lot to do with the conversion.

Some examples:

> The Phillies pitcher had *[filthy]* stuff all night long.
>
> We had *[ridiculous]* seats at the US Open. Right down at courtside.
>
> These people are paying *[stupid]* amounts of money to see the fight.
>
> Cooper's one-handed catch and throw back to second was *[sick]*.
>
> LeBron is flat-out *[freakish]* when he gets the ball under the net.

Pay attention to these catchy, unorthodox language trends. Bring them into your writing when you need to. They're fresh, topical, and they hook specific readers. It pays to learn when and how to use them.

INNOVATE!

*Styles showed a **freakish** talent for making our sales figures dance for the shareholders. His PowerPoint presentation got **ridiculous** amounts of positive feedback from participants.*

Granted, sometimes you may even have to see yourself almost as a pop culture vandal, engaged in drive-by word lifting.

That's OK, because **boldness wins**.

> "Words are instruments, they are tools that, in their different ways, are as effective as any sharp edge or violate chemical. They are, like coins, items of great value, but they represent a currency that, well spent, return ever greater riches."
>
> —*Tim Radford*—

SENTENCES: LEADING THE CONVERSATION

A first commandment: Use declarative sentences. They work.

Bold statements are dangerous, but they won't kill you. Timidity, or softness, will.

> *Sam's technical knowledge and Samantha's people skills make a killer combination for us. We need to get these folks in front of the customer.*
>
> *We know we have the best solution for the customer. Let's go with it.*

Sure, everyone has a hazy opinion or two, but why would you ever want to ask an already reluctant reader to put your intentions to a multiple choice test?

SET THE RHYTHM OF THE DANCE

Parallel structure creates a sense of rhythm within a sentence or paragraph, between paragraphs, or in a bulleted list. Parallelism means using the same sentence structure for related topics, like starting each sentence in a paragraph with a verb, or each item in a bulleted list with an adjective.

One form of parallelism uses word combinations that have *balanced sounds, syllable counts, placement,* or *meaning*—like this one, from the world of advertising:

> *Denny—*
> *You'll like the design of our new chassis assembly prototype, especially the way it's **packed, stacked, and backed**. I'll give you a call this afternoon to bring you up to speed on the marketing pitch we're planning. –Kristen*

Another form of parallelism repeats key words, messages, or phrases.

Easy to buy, easy to install, easy to use, and easy to expand.

Or, you can use combinations of repeated words and phrases to create a sense of steady rhythm.

"We want to take it out of beta. We want to move it to production. We want to bring it to market."

EXPERIMENT!

TRY THIS: Plant some test balloons in your next email, report, or other suitable product. Then pay attention to the outcome. But a word of caution here: You have to know how much is enough. <u>Too</u> much repetition can weaken the potency of your delivery.

CONTROL THE DIALOGUE

Here's a new type of semantic for controlling the dialogue: "*Well, look.*" We hear it more and more lately, especially from political candidates on the campaign trail, or guest subject matter experts on CNN.

What are you doing when you introduce this kind of command at the outset of your conversation? You're <u>forcing</u> your readers to pay attention. You're telling them to wait for instructions on what to do next.

And you know what? Most of the time, *they do!*

The construction is simple and effective. You lead with your imperative word or phrase, and then you immediately follow up with your main point.

Look. *Everybody's falling in line behind our competition. We need to take the campaign in a new, fresher direction. Now.*

Listen. There's never been a better time to take advantage of this opportunity to bring our brand to a larger arena.

Think about it. Do we really want to give up a seat at the decision table because we're not in agreement on the best path forward for our campaign?

Not so fast. If we charge down that path without factoring in all the risks, we're setting ourselves up for failure.

Guess again. On the surface it may look like an obvious choice, but our research is telling us something else.

Believe it. Nobody has the magic formula for increasing our sales 20% by this time next year. It's going to take a lot of hard work by all of us to get there.

Pull your reader into the conversation.

USE STRONG DIRECTIONAL CUES

Directional cues channel your reader's attention, giving you tactical command of the situation. Here are some ways the technique can be used:

<statement>. **But remember:** *<directing/qualifying statement>*

Sure, we can pursue that market segment. *But remember:* It's new territory for us.

<statement>. **If you do, know this:** *<assertion>*

You can add that requirement to the request for proposals. *If you do, know this:* There's a finite number of bidders out there who can meet our needs.

<directing statement>. **be sure to keep in mind** *<further directing text>*

OK. Take the risk and bring that consultant team onboard. When you do, *be sure to keep in mind* their core expertise will have to be beefed up in certain areas.

ANOTHER GOOD CONTROL TACTIC

I call this one the "Rumsfeld Method." National political figures and public servants like former Defense Secretary Donald Rumsfeld get a lot of mileage out of this little gambit. They use it when they find themselves in the unenviable position of having to defend controversial policy decisions before an increasingly hostile press.

It's a straightforward technique. State the issue and then immediately pose a question:

> *Our market share looks good today, but we don't know what product demand will be when those new regulations take effect next quarter. Should we cover our bases?*
>
> *Absolutely. But at the same time, we shouldn't pull back on our aggressive sales campaign.*

What's the value of this strategy? It shapes the direction of the conversation and moves the dialogue down a path <u>you</u> control.

ADDITION BY SUBTRACTION: KEEP SENTENCES SHORT

Reader confusion and disconnects are much more likely in longer sentences. So keep your constructions simple. Don't try to do too much.

Nothing's worse than huffing and puffing through a bunch of filler words that try unsuccessfully to bridge a subject and verb.

Wield a ruthless scalpel and cut, cut, **CUT**.

- Chunk like topics together.
- Get in the habit of splitting what would otherwise be long sentences.
- Bring your reader to the <u>period</u> as soon as possible.

> *"If it is possible to cut a word out, always cut it out."*
> —George Orwell—

BUILD CADENCE INTO YOUR SENTENCES

Words march to a beat. Sentences have a rhythm. Their pace can be fast or slow; their cadence, smooth or quick-chop, staccato. Skillful writers learn how to control the rhythm and tempo their words dance to, by varying the structure of their sentences.

Just don't be predictable. When readers are used to looking at a steady diet of fast balls, it's nice to get a change-up now and then.

> **RULE OF THUMB:** *Longer sentences can flow gently, picking up momentum as they go. Short sentences create a tense, insistent rhythm. Repetition adds accent and meter.*

USE TRANSITION WORDS TO CHANNEL ATTENTION

Transition words are your navigators. They're located at the beginning of a sentence and they lead your readers (your <u>consumers</u>, remember?) in the direction you want them to go. The right words will help carry forward a main idea, signal a shift of thought, the start of a contrasting perspective, or sum up and crystalize a conclusion.

Specific writing objectives call for specific transition techniques.

Some examples:

> **For continuing a common line of reasoning**: *what's more, given that, clearly, on top of that, plus, in the same way, taking this a step further, from here, it's easy to see that, when you look at it that way*

> **To signal a shift in a line of reasoning** (contrast) or to counter or override a prevailing mindset: *on the flip side, on the other hand, going the opposite way, despite all of that, nevertheless*

For opening a paragraph or for general use: *admittedly, no doubt, without question, at this level, in this situation, nobody denies, unquestionably, to be sure*

To underscore a final point: *bottom line, in a nutshell, to wrap it all up, let's recap, here's what we're left with*

For transitional chains, to separate sections of a paragraph that's arranged chronologically: *first...second...third; for starters...furthermore...finally; in the first place...taking this a step further...to conclude*

To restate a point within a paragraph in another way or in a more exacting way: *put another way, in other words, that is, point in fact, to clarify*

To guide your reader through a sequence of time: *afterwards, before long, as soon as, at last, in the first place, meanwhile, next, in the meantime*

Get the idea? Use transition words to strengthen your *middle game*. They're connecting devices you deploy to build and sustain momentum, bolster your case, and steer your reader to your tactical conclusion.

Then, when you've tied it all together and made your point, **close the deal**.

No:

> *Let me know how I can assist you. — Kim*

Yes:

> *I'm here to help. Contact me any time and I'll get you answers to any remaining questions or concerns. And I'll follow up with you within a few days just to make sure we're tracking. — Kim*

Never leave anything open ended.

SENTENCE IMPERATIVES: SUMMING IT UP

- Use strong sentence openings with a call to action that matters. No second thoughts. No wasting time. No hesitation.

- Answer your reader's "*So what?*" objection with every sentence you write.

- **Ask for what you want**, without using any hedging words and phrases like "*if*" and "*perhaps*."

- Use "you" and "your" to make (and keep) a personal connection with your reader.

- Use **energetic** language.

    SIDE NOTE: *The word "that" almost automatically weakens a sentence. Even worse, it makes the writer sound stiff, unnatural. Go through every bit of writing you do and cut out the word "that" as many times as you can. Sometimes it's not easy, because the word is everywhere. But stay diligent.*

- Make sure someone, or something, is performing some action in as many of your sentences as possible.

And don't be afraid to use fragments. When they reflect clear, simple language, you can use a varied, careful mix of longer sentences, shorter sentences, and, yes, fragments.

PARAGRAPHS: HOLDING IT ALL TOGETHER

Always aim for strong, quick, *killer paragraphs*.

Your reader has to take in every single word you write. Not just the bullets. Not just the first sentences. *Every single word.* You can't afford to have them skimming and skipping around in your paragraphs looking for the "meat." It had better all be meat.

> **UNCHANGING TRUTH:** *Readers will read if it's worth their time. Killer paragraphs make that happen.*

Somebody once said good paragraphs leave no sentence behind. Believe it. The purpose of the first sentence is to get your reader to the second sentence. And the sole function of the second sentence is to get your reader to move on to the third sentence. And so on.

If there's any sentence in a paragraph that isn't connected to what came before it—isn't logically and systematically getting people to read the next one—get rid of it.

TWO MORE MUST-DOs...

- Use paragraphs to form chains of thought that won't be broken.

- Know when to end. Every paragraph should last long enough to make **one single point**. When your point is made, move on to the next paragraph — and your next point.

ASK THE RIGHT QUESTIONS

Questions are an effective technique for opening and closing your message. Use questions to prompt your reader to take a look at a problem through your eyes and reconsider a competitive viewpoint. This tactic works best when the questions are directed to the reader or when they're written from the reader's perspective.

Would it be better if the unemployment rate were 5%? Of course it would. But a 5% unemployment rate might also mean those unsuited for labor are being pressed into service. A low rate like that could be an indicator of a government out of control.

The rhetorical question guides a reader (or listener) along a predetermined path of "logic." Pastors and religious leaders use it all the time. Politicians depend on it. (Refer back to *"The Rumsfeld Method"* to see what I mean.)

What's more, using first or second person in your questions enhances reader buy-in and increases your chances of encouraging them to continue on, to discover the answer—*your* answer.

Some of the best writing drops in questions throughout, to build a case gradually. Used sparingly, it works. But again, be aware: Like anything else, when used to excess, the tactic becomes annoying.

STIR WITH IMAGERY

It's always easier to get a reader to come around to your way of thinking when you take a new or highly technical product or issue and describe it in a familiar way. You can make this happen by using imagery techniques, like *analogy* and *metaphor*.

Here's a high-level overview:

Analogy – "It's like this.."

ANALOGY suggests *a likeness between two things* based on similar or shared attributes. It's a useful convention for emphasizing the special characteristics of a product, service, or activity.

> *To call this marketing campaign a battle*
> *is like saying D-Day was a skirmish.*

Here, you're using analogy to underscore a point by making a literal, concrete comparison of things belonging to the same class (battle and D-Day are both combat-related terms). You can also use analogy to make a figurative comparison of two completely different things:

> Heather —
> *Our customers in the more remote areas of the county are getting fed up with waiting for things to get better. Like the owners of starter homes that have become too small for growing families, many of these subscribers think their local dial-up Internet phone service is doing a lousy job in keeping up with their exploding need for speedier web access.*

Use analogy when you want to compare things based on a relationship of one-to-one, one-to-many, many-to-one, or many-to-many.

Metaphor – "This is THAT..."

METAPHOR implies a comparison by using symbolism or describing a technical idea or feature in terms of something non-technical. This method draws its effectiveness from ***showing your reader something in a new light*** or describing something complex in simpler, more familiar terms.

Like this:

> An Ivy League economist was attempting to explain what happens when two large companies merge. He talked about the difficulties of combining the different cultures, business practices, information technology systems, and standards. The presentation moved along as a kind of left brain, dry explanation of what happens when two companies combine, emphasizing the main point that the whole process is difficult. But he nailed it when he closed with this assertion:

"Bottom-line: When elephants mate, you don't get Bambi."

Now that's a provocative leave-behind—one that readers won't easily forget. They might forget some specific facts, but they'll never forget the speaker's key point.

Remember: When you go with a metaphor, you have to use symbolism in a way your audience can recognize and interpret correctly (i.e., the way you want them to).

History is a struggle of the memory.
Pain is weakness leaving the body.

Lively, provocative examples of metaphors can be found in current events, sports, entertainment, music, nature, or hobbies. Remember, with metaphor, you're comparing things in a one-to-one relationship. Collect examples that click with you—and use them.

CHECK OUT:
http://www.visualthesaurus.com/cm/candlepwr/business-communicators-got-metaphor/ for more good information on using metaphor in business writing.

HOOK AND HOLD

Don't forget: Your goal is to seize your reader's attention and hold it hostage long enough to finish the job. That means your first sentence is key. It sets the stage for everything that follows.

Try these tactics to emphasize action—right from the start.

THE DIRECT ADDRESS (IMPERATIVE) - Implies the second person without using the pronoun "you." This kind of declarative, commanding lead draws your reader right into the action flow.

It muscles your way in. (You're in control, remember?)

Forget what the industry analysts are reporting. The only question now is, "How strong of a response have we made to the voice of our customer as it was communicated to us through our last satisfaction survey?" A quick look at our follow-up actions to date screams out the answer loud and clear: "Not very."

THE INFINITIVE LEAD - Starts off with "To" followed by a power verb. This method emphasizes *directed action*.

To capture and understand the true meaning of where we are with market share, don't watch where we are on the ticker tape. Watch who's watching us on the ticker tape.

THE PUNCH, QUICK KICK, OR TWIST - Leads with a short, snappy sentence set off by itself. A summary of supporting details comes in right behind the punch. Use this opening when you have one fact that's over-the-top important, or a main point you want to emphasize with a twist ending.

Start with a high-startle attention freeze:

Brian —

Something's way out of whack here.

Nobody's called us to complain about late deliveries. Our customer service desk is picking up phone calls on the first ring. Our turnover rate has gone down steadily for the last six months. Everyone on the team is going the extra mile to help each other out.

Where did this crowd come from and what have they done with our company?

Or open with a **big-hand assertion** to feed curiosity and force reader engagement:

Janice —

You could go all the way to retirement without ever getting pulled into a conference call like the one we had yesterday.

57

THE QUESTION - Starts off by asking the obvious. But it's often best to use this one as a last resort.

> *Bill —*
>
> *How can something as inexpensive as paper clips have such a crippling impact on our bottom line? I'm not kidding. It's a question that's been driving our Finance people bonkers for the past year. And now guess who was picked to run this thing to ground.*

CARDINAL RULE: DO <u>NOT</u> PROJECT "INCOMPETENT"

Remember, you're aiming to project *powerful, confident,* and *professional.*

- Nothing shouts "*amateur!*" like embedded, ungrammatical word bombs in the first sentence of your product (or anywhere else in the communication, for that matter).
- You'd better know the difference between words like *effect/affect, farther/further,* and *it's/its.*

> **TIP:** Read "30 Incorrectly Used Words That Can Make You Look Horrible": *http://time.com/96982/incorrectly-used-words/*

Believe it. Nothing decimates credibility like sentences and paragraphs that read like they were ham-handed out by a high school dropout (just sayin').

PS: Don't be too proud (or self-assured) to ask for another set of eyeballs on your product before you launch. Even the most talented writers are smart enough to know their work can only benefit from a sanity check before it goes out the door.

> *"On Twitter, people respect you for sharing your deepest, darkest flaws. Unless those flaws are typos, in which case, die in a fire."*
> —Louis C.K.—

BIG FINISH

Let's review:

- Your *language* must be potent, expressive, and easy to understand.

- Your *phrasing* must follow the natural, using varied rhythms of speech.

- Your *words, sentences,* and *paragraphs* must work together in seamless harmony to secure reader buy-in for your controlling idea.

- You <u>must</u> know what you want out of every single writing engagement. *Break it down.*

- You must keep your strategy nimble. Don't be back on your heels. Stay on your toes—and project *action.*

These are the components of a *Full Contact Writing* mindset.

BONUS ADVICE: While you're preparing to move down this exciting path of *do-it-now* writing, take these two additional action items with you…

1. read. Read. **READ**.

Read everything about the craft of writing you can get your hands on. Look through books, magazines, articles. Everything. (I've included a list of some good ones in the back of this book, under *More Tools for Writers*.) Don't stop educating yourself. Heck, read all kinds of stuff.

2. **Clip and save** good ads, illustrations, words on signs, great junk mail, newspaper content, etc.

It's worth repeating: When you come across strong content—on and offline writing that connects with you and rings a bell—cut it out and put it in your working notebook. Be a string saver.

What does all this do for you, besides improve your writing skills?

- It forces you to capture and synthesize *best practices* into your writing style.
- You start to become aware of the *motivational factors* behind words.
- You begin *formalizing things you did instinctively*, understanding how and why writing works at a more conceptual level.

In other words, not only do your writing mechanics get better, but your understanding of the subtleties and power of wordsmithing gets much more tangible.

Besides, "evolving" and "adapting" are no longer optional parts of a competitive business writing and communication strategy. They go to the core of your success in the world of work—and beyond.

If you've been paying attention this far, you're on your way to becoming a word warrior in the *Full Contact Writing* arena.

And you know something? It's *exciting*.

> "No profit grows where no pleasure is taken."

Good luck and happy hunting!

YOUR NEXT STEP: JUMP IN AND SWIM!

There you go. You have the essential components for building your power writing platform. I've given you the elements of a win system that works—a collection of simple approaches that deliver consistent, positive outcomes. I've shown you how to **ACE** it.

Now **put it all together**. You have the foundation, the basics. In the following sections, we'll look at how you can fine-tune them.

> *"Vigorous writing is concise. A sentence should contain no unnecessary words, a paragraph no unnecessary sentences, for the same reason that a drawing should have no unnecessary lines and a machine no unnecessary parts. This requires not that the writer make all his sentences short, or that he avoid all detail and treat his subjects only in outline, but that every word tell."*
>
> *—William Strunk Jr.—*
> The Elements of Style

WRITING IN ACTION: NOTES FROM THE PROVING GROUND

> *"I put things down on sheets of paper and stuff them in my pockets. When I have enough, I have a book."*
> —John Lennon—

In coming up with the idea for this book, it was like that for me. Every writing challenge I helped somebody else overcome became an entry in my gold book of lessons learned. All of those hints, tips, and informal "experiments" that worked were tagged, bagged, and locked in the vault.

Not surprisingly, along the way I discovered quite a few speed bumps that even the most experienced writers trip over from time to time.

The snippets of ACE-based guidance in this section will help you anticipate and overcome these obstacles. Use the input that follows to augment your Full Contact Writing playbook.

Think of it as field notes from the proving ground.

> **QUICK CAVEAT:** *The topics included here are in no way meant to be taken as exhaustive. They're offered as additional (and informal) "applied wisdom." They're useful because they address some of the main, workhorse writing most of us generate on a daily basis.*

Go back to these pages when you need to. And while you're at it, keep adding more *win examples* to your tool box as you grow in your writing success.

ALWAYS WRITE TO WIN

Writing to win is <u>your</u> responsibility—so don't get lazy.

Even if your job description says nothing about writing, you need to regard yourself as a writer, at least privately. That means cultivating the healthiest level of respect for the written word and its importance in business.

HEY! This is a golden opportunity for you, so pay attention. People in corporate America have to know how to articulate their ideas, accomplishments, and expectations. More often than not, this happens in an **email**, where a simple turn of a phrase, or engaging attention to detail and tone, sends a powerful first, second, and even *third* impression.

Successful writers know their email message <u>provokes</u> when they're true to the right style.

> **REPEAT: DO NOT GET LAZY.** *Thanks to the often brutal, unforgiving immediacy of emails and instant messaging, the minute we hit SEND, our words are nowhere in space, yet everywhere at once.*

This reality calls for a word of caution and awareness. When we think we're writing to one person, our words are frequently forwarded to many. So it's a two-edged sword. We're broadening our influence, but at the same time we're exposed to a larger, less-defined circle of readers, each with special biases and agendas.

> *"Your brand is what people say about you when you're not in the room."*
> —*Jeff Bezos, Amazon.com* —

So remember: Whenever you write, you're guaranteed a speedy trial in the court of public opinion.

BOTTOM LINE: Neglecting, or losing sight of the image you're projecting as a writer carries severe consequences.

Case in point:

> *A line-level IT manager gets the word from her boss, a senior director, that her yearly bonus will be slashed by 50%, because she hasn't taken the time to improve the quality of her written communication skills, as evidenced by her weak, ineffective, and error-prone emails. Others in (and outside) the department cringe when they're on the receiving end of this stuff.*

Yep. This really happened. It happens all the time.

Anybody you know?

PROTECT YOUR REPUTATION

Trust me. You don't ever want to fall into the trap of just sending out words. An email, a broadcast bulletin, or a service proposal that transmits disorganized ideas, tired wording, faulty constructions, or grammatical blow-ups tells your reader volumes about you.

Here's an email I received when I was working on a proposal team for a large IT services company:

> *Team,*
>
> *As of 1600, 9 Jan 2009, we have not gotten official word of an extension. However, unofficially, we have beliefs that the Government will give a two weeks extension which makes the due date 30 Jan 2009.*
>
> *It could be longer, but to date we believe no shorter. Our decision was to No-Bid if earlier than 6 Feb 2009. The one week difference between 30 Jan and 6 Feb is critical to the success of our collective efforts.*
>
> *Having said that, I welcome your inputs on if we are extended through 30 Jan 2009, do you believe we can get this done in the allotted time?*

> *We have yet to receive inputs from a couple of the Team members and believe what we have seen, justifies the Teams Composition and respective capabilities. The question is can we get this done by 30 Jan 2009?*
>
> *We can discuss on Monday, if the status of no Government response remains as is today. However, we will need to begin work on preparing our Technical response.*
>
> *Thoughts?*
>
> *Bill*

"Bill" acted alone in this message assassination. There were no accomplices.

How many times does writing like this make its way to your inbox in a day? A week? A *year?* If you're the writer here, why would you allow yourself to be a victim, if you didn't have to be?

DON'T FORGET: Your words move out before you, like your foot soldiers, meeting the unknown head-on.

> *The truest measure of a company isn't size. It's substance. A point of view exemplified by Sage Software's more than 2.3 million North American customers. These hard-working businesses range from start-ups to budding global enterprises. They share one thing in common. They want their businesses to succeed.*
>
> *Sage Software, part of The Sage Group plc, has been helping in that cause for 25 years. We build innovative software solutions. Powerful solutions. Intelligent solutions. Solutions that help people face the challenges of running a small or midsized business. The kinds of challenges they can't stop thinking about even when they're not at the office. We understand what's in their hearts and on their minds. Because we talk to them. And listen.*
>
> *We've proven ourselves in their distribution warehouses and on their manufacturing floors. At their construction sites. In their nonprofit organizations. But our journey*

never truly ends, it merely evolves. So do we, with software that offers more than functionality. Much more. Our solutions are flexible. Affordable. Integrated. They are inspired by the people who use them. Not the latest fads. They are built to meet the needs, challenges, and dreams of businesses and organizations like yours. And they are defined by the most important measure of all: your satisfaction.

—Sage Software (online company brochure)—

Now that's what I'm talking about.

Writing in business is a battleground. And it should be. Your task as a writer is to **make the conflict fruitful**.

SYSTEM FAILURE: NOT SO TRANSPARENT TO THE USER

Were you ever watching a movie when you noticed a scene where the film editor screwed up and a technical flaw appeared, right there on screen? You know, where the fuzzy tip of the sound microphone is dangling over the actor, during a living room conversation, or the guy's hair is parted on the right side in the first close-up and then on the left side in the next shot? There was an obvious breakdown in the logical flow, the natural rhythm of events.

You were on the receiving end. You saw it. And it bothered you.

The shift from the printed word to the Internet has taken us from a culture of memory to a **CULTURE OF ATTENTION**. And in this new world order you never notice something until it stops working the way it's supposed to—or the way you expect it to.

How many times have you come across an email, letter, resume, or other written product that was so poorly done, or so obviously kluged and cobbled together, with no regard for results? What did you do after you finished reading it (assuming you finished)? You probably formed an impression of the sender that, uh, wasn't so flattering. Then, you no doubt deleted it without a second thought.

Stock <u>down</u> for that writer.

The new normal? Maybe not yet, but we're heading in that direction.

I'll tell it like it is. I'm convinced most people who (under duress) write in the business world don't see themselves as writers. Consequently, they don't take full ownership of their product.

Not surprisingly then, they have no idea of the full range of possibilities for success their words can generate—even in the most routine situations. What's more, they often fail to understand that writing today is an exercise in *identity management*.

Seriously, how much is your corporate identity worth to you? When you write, make it count, because you're being judged.

> *"I have offered ideas to improve communication toward work flow and status, but none have been implemented."*
> —(excerpt from the self-assessment portion of an employee's annual performance review)—

Writers like this, who stay stuck in neutral, will always get beat up like a piñata.

Stay strong. Stay positive. Anything you write counts. Every memo, update, letter, budget request—they all build impressions with your reader.

> **FACT:** *There's no place for sissies when it comes to dealing with that shape-shifting target called "audience."*

It's all about the long ball. It's about power.

We like it. We should.

FORCING FUNCTION AND WRITING TO MOVE

By anybody's estimation, Curt Schilling was a stud pitcher. His performance at Yankee Stadium in game 6 of the 2004 American League Championship series could rank among the most courageous in sports history. I mean, stitching up his ankle so he can pitch? He was a monster. "A Frankenstein with a fastball," as one writer called him.

That's what you want people to say about you and your skill with words. Why not aim high?

Just wanting to reach that level of "**wow!**" will put you on a track that's out ahead of the crowd. That's because way too much writing isn't getting past "So *what?*" (Given this stark reality, you might say we need more cops on the beat to cut down on the number of victims.)

Here's the thing. When you get right down to it, most breakdowns happen because there's no psychological or pressure shift—or what's called a **Forcing Function**—behind much of the written communication moving through the workplace channels.

A forcing function comes out of the world of project management, and it's anything that naturally forces a change in perspective, attitude, or behavior.

> SIDE NOTE: For a great study on communication, decision-making, and mind-game strategy in the world of business, check out Scott Berkun's *The Art of Project Management*, O'Reilly Media, 2005.

Make sure every piece of writing you generate contains a built-in forcing function. This means you're always out to get velocity behind your words. In Extreme Programming, *velocity* refers to a program's probable performance, based on previous performance (Berkun again). Once again, this simple principle applies to your writing. If a particular strategy worked well once, the chances are good it will work again.

Repeatable action = Consistent outcome.

THE BEST WAY TO DRAIN POWER FROM YOUR WRITING PUNCH? LEAD WITH YOUR CHIN

One of the best ways I know of to kill the win potential of your business writing is to deliver sentences with wimp openings. We're all guilty from time to time of throwing in these milk toast starts to what otherwise could (and should) be clear, concise assertions.

Wimp openings are static words that sit on the fence and do nothing to advance an agenda, cement an argument, or nail down a point. Instead, they reinforce reader perception of a writer who hasn't yet made a decision. Like a baseball player who got caught looking at a third strike, with his bat sitting on his shoulder.

Negative perceptions die a lonely death in the world of work.

Look at some of these examples. (Hint: the culprits are in brackets.)

[I believe] we should proceed with a sense of cautious optimism that consumer demand will turn around in the next quarter.

[I think] conditions are right for an aggressive push to capture the data that will help us substantiate our goals for new business development in that market space.

[For what it's worth], here's my position on that hot button topic we touched on at the meeting.

[Maybe] we should solicit the help of our consultant team to move this agenda item forward.

I'll [try to] stay focused on these trends and report back to you with any changes in market direction.

[It's possible that] we're setting ourselves up for disappointment if we move ahead on this project without going through our due diligence.

Then look at the strong, on-point tone each of these sentences takes on when you <u>delete</u> the baggage.

Other variations on the theme: *attempt, imagine, suppose, guess…*

> **CHECK OUT:** *"Six Phrases to Avoid if You Want to be Taken Seriously at Work"*
> http://www.businessinsider.com/what-not-to-say-at-work-2013-10

> *"I may be wrong, but I am never in doubt."*
> *—Marshall McLuhan—*

And why would you ever start with a "hopefully" and end with an open-ended "wondering" like this writer did:

> *From: FIFE, BARNEY*
> *Sent: Monday, September 10, 2012 11:21 AM*
> *To: DONUTS, JOE BAG*
> *Cc: CARUSO, ROBINSON*
> *Subject: Test Development*
>
> *Morning Joe,*
>
> *Hopefully you're aware that we're building an employee incentive program to improve the motivation and efficiency of our work force. Our goal right now is to try to complete three unique phases leading up to program rollout: Survey, Planning, and Implementation. Wondering if you could assist in this endeavor?*
>
> *Thanks.*
> *Barney*

OK. This example may be grammatically correct and (seemingly) well written. But, in baseball terms, it's an "empty hit." It failed to score any runs.

REWRITE.

FIVE SAY-NOTHING PHRASES TO QUICKSAND NOW: GO AHEAD—YOU KNOW YOU WANT TO...

An email I received some time ago was the last straw. It was from a former colleague of mine. He was out to sell me on the idea of pursuing some new business in a market space that didn't exactly line up with our company's core services. I had to give him credit. This guy was in there pitching. Problem was, he managed to trot out many of the tired, worn-out phrases that had long since made their way to my "Kill" folder.

Did it bother me to have to trip over them again in this email? Big time. So much so that I sent him a reply, with the offenders highlighted—and I asked him to clarify!

Here they are:

>1. **Move the needle**. "*He was barely able to move the needle with his presentation.*" What? Was he strapped to a polygraph machine? This one's flat-lined. Besides, we're digital now, remember?

>2. **Take it to a whole new level**. "*If we get in on this opportunity, it will take our operations to a whole new level.*" Really? How will I know when I've arrived? Sounds like you're building a stairway to heaven.

>3. **Get us out of our comfort zone**. "*Partnering with these guys will force us to get out of our comfort zone, take more strategic chances, and reap greater reward.*" Comfort zone. I like comfort. Who doesn't? Why would I want to bail on comfort?

>4. **Raise the bar**. "*Their CEO has raised the bar on timely response to customer inquiries.*" I love this one. Makes me think I'm a pole vaulter in a track and field meet and they just made it tougher for me to grab a medal.

>5. **Bump it up a notch**. No words needed here.

We see and hear phrases like this more often than we want to. At one time they may have been perceived as edgy or cool, with writers bringing them positive buzz.

But many times buzz bounces are like ice cream cones: soft, sweet, and they melt in five minutes.

> **CHECK OUT:**
> "*The Six Words That Are Holding You Back*"
> http://www.entrepreneur.com/article/234488

NUKE THESE OLD WRITING MYTHS!

"First, your return to shore was not part of our negotiations nor our agreement, so I must do nothin'. And secondly, you must be a pirate for the Pirate's Code to apply, and you're not. And thirdly, the Code is more what you'd call 'guidelines' than actual rules. Welcome aboard the Black Pearl, Miss Turner."
—Captain Barbossa—
(*from the film* Pirates of the Caribbean:
The Curse of the Black Pearl)

Certain myths must be destroyed. Especially writing myths. In a sense, today's business world is the *Black Pearl*, and if we're part of that corporate jungle, we're onboard.

Ours is a world where everything's negotiable—even when it comes to how you choose to deal with those draconian do-it-this-way writing "guidelines."

So…moving ahead with our out with the old, in with the new scheme, here are a few old-school writing codes of conduct that have outlived their usefulness. They don't even warrant the rank of "guidelines" anymore. **Lose them**.

- Never start a sentence with *but, so, because, and,* or *however*.

    So why not? **Because** English teachers working from a 1950s book on grammar said so? No coloring outside the lines? This one's dead for all kinds of reasons.

- Never put a comma before "*and*."

    A comma before *and* may, in fact, help the reader to see how the sentence is constructed, **and** it can put a pause exactly where you want it, for effect.

- Never end a sentence with a preposition.

    Most of us have been chastised for this one. Die-hard grammarians like to jump on this no-no like a loose football. Truth is, this outdated rule of thumb just isn't something you can hang your hat **on**.

- Never split your infinitives.

    Does this "never do" look like a devastating, automatic chain mover? Not exactly. If you think a sentence will pack more punch, or achieve greater clarity or rhythm, go ahead, split your infinitive. There's no reason in logic or grammar for avoiding it.

- Never write a one-sentence paragraph.

    If this is the answer I'd hate to see the question. Whenever you can say what you want to say in a single sentence that lacks a direct connection with any other sentence, just stop there and go on to a new paragraph.

    There's nothing to stop you.

- You should always test your writing with a readability formula before you send it.

    Really? E=MC2 for writers. Let me know when you find a "readability" formula that works for you. Without fail. <u>Every</u> time you need it to.

YOU CAN'T SAY THAT AGAIN…

Cutting away the dead wood can be fun—and *rewarding*. Let's keep going. Here are more words and phrases you can send packing—once and for all. They're fluff, they're sterile, and they yield <u>zero</u> return on your (time) investment.

Enclosed please find
Prioritize
Pursuant to your request
Strategize
It has come to my attention
Supposedly
Maybe
I guess

> *Perhaps*
> *ASAP*
> *Please advise*
> *Please do not hesitate to contact me*
> *Dear Sir or Madam*
> *Very unique*
> *To whom it may concern*
> *Thank you in advance for your cooperation*
> *As yet undetermined*
> *At some level*
> *At the end of the day*

Stay on the hunt for more examples to add to this list. Like these: *just, really, very, literally, honestly, actually, quite.*

Bankrupt placeholders like these are the mortal enemies of **FULL CONTACT WRITING.**

"NETERATURE" AND YOU

Here's something else to keep in mind. Online, anyone who types can be a "writer." In theory, that is. Blogs, comments, social media bursts, news filterese, spam poetry, prose parodies. The wonderful worldwide web has opened the floodgates for everybody and anybody to splash their words out to every corner of the global village.

The result? There's this deep undercurrent of quirky, jerky writing online. I heard a term for it that sticks with me: *"Neterature."*

Neterature is a word that's come to mean writing on and for the Internet.

We all know it when we see it. It's writing that's:

- Not always in complete sentences

- Often stacked with bullets—and little else

- Not a lot of punctuation but a great deal of "self-exploration" like, you know, whatever…

- case often upper when should be lower and Vice Versa
- Rife with misteaks—easily corrected but mor often not
- Full of attitude and not always happy. Sometimes cynical and sinister, and loaded with obscenities, Other times it's over the top with winking, smiley-face emoticons that are "lol'ing" at everything.

Neterature: It's energetic, passionate, innovative, and irreverently funny. Often seen as not always great or even good. But the best of it is young and edgy and full of life, in ways that more traditional writing isn't so much anymore.

And it's alive and mutating—in email and instant messages, even spilling off the screen into our daily conversation. It's generated by and for groups connected by some common interests or affiliations.

More to the point, it's changing the way we express ourselves. People are writing shorter, and they're leading readers to other sites through clickable links.

In this marketplace, the fear is always that people will jump away from your message and not come back.

Flash: The fear is justified. People do jump, so new forms of "grabby" writing are springing up.

    GRABBY WRITING. That's what you're after.

PRACTICE THE ART OF PERSUASION

"'The purpose of communication is persuasion.' I heard this aphorism in one of those management improvement sessions (at a resort hotel) that the contemporary corporation uses so extensively, to 'improve communications,' among other reasons. It has haunted me ever since. For what it says is that there is no point in mere transfer of cognitive knowledge of information, no point in journalistic or scientific reporting…Communication becomes a strategy of power, a model of 'winning friends and influencing people.' Its enemy is not misunderstanding or ignorance but improper attitudes and values."—Wilbert E. Moore, The Conduct of the Corporation—

IT'S WORDS THAT SELL—EVERYTHING

The formula sounds simple: It doesn't matter whether your words push out from an oversized monitor and bounce across your reader's eyeballs, or they make a soft landing on somebody's desk, via snail mail, as print on pulp. To achieve more, write better.

Make the most productive use of your words. The right words, assembled and packaged correctly, will overcome the largest obstacles. But launch the wrong words, in the wrong context, and even your most critical business agenda is toast. You'll get tarred by whatever brush is out there.

Pretty serious stuff, especially when so many people in the work place tell themselves...

*"***I am not a writer***."*

In all fairness, most people aren't. Thomas Pynchon is a writer. Stephen King is a writer. Writing is about crafting captivating fiction, stories about the human condition. Tales of loss and redemption.

These are literary writers. They're people we think of as literary greats, like Ernest Hemingway—who, by the way, did have some great advice for us writers in the workplace. (Check out some of his tips at the end of this book. It's practical wisdom every *Full Contact Writer* should follow.)

> **HERE'S MY POINT**. *Stop blaming your pre-conceived lack of ability for why you're not a better writer. It's a convenient excuse, which also happens to be false.*

Now, back quickly to the live-or-die proposition of email. The health of your entire span of relationships with coworkers or customers often rests solely on your email exchanges. You may head up a $20 million project without ever meeting your coworkers or client face-to-face. Yet these unseen faces in the crowd (your crowd) are out there.

They're waiting for your email—waiting to be told where, when, why, or how you want them to do something (and, of course, what they can expect to get in return).

> **HEADS UP:** Check out *ChangingMinds.org*, the largest site in the world on all aspects of how we change what others think, believe, feel, and do. There are over 7000 pages available through this site, all free.

MORE NOTES ON PERSUASIVE LANGUAGE

Persuasion calls for language with impact: it's graphic and it's out to create an emotional charge. Barriers to this emotional charge (and the ways to overcome them) include:

Distance (create the illusion of immediate presence)

Time (make the issues exist in the here-and-now)

Apathy (stimulate your jaded audience with new insights, humor, or graphic detail)

Persuasive language is anchored in the present moment. It's not remote or abstract.

"Just do it!"—Nike

What's more, persuasive writing takes into account the connotations—the <u>emotional</u> content—of words, not just their denotation, or dictionary definitions.

And (brace yourself) persuasion isn't primarily concerned with truth. It's more about *motivation*. You're prodding somebody to do something and your only focus is on making that happen.

So be clear in what you're asking. This one seems obvious, but sometimes readers don't take action, not because you lack persuasive powers, but because they aren't sure how to move forward.

Be certain there's no possible disconnect with what you're asking, how to get started, and what comes next. It may be your reader wants to be onboard—but isn't sure how to climb on. What's clear to you may not be clear at all.

PUSH BENEFITS, NOT FEATURES

Always, always, **ALWAYS** emphasize benefits over features. Your readers could care less how many bells and whistles you're writing about. They want to know what you're going to do for them.

> **Feature:** *Mike—This widget has three new monitoring capabilities—system security diagnostics, a backup power source, and a thermostat controller.*
>
> **Benefit:** *Mike—If you buy this widget with its three new monitoring capabilities, we can all finally go relax on a vacation. This smart device works while the team is freed up to do other things. It's a worry-free proposition—the widget makes sure our internal security system is online and operational, our power source is backed up, and the temperature of our facility is maintained at a constant, fuel-saving level.*

THE BINDS THAT TIE

Binds create the *illusion of choice* by using language that normally offers at least two options. But no matter what choice readers make, they will still be going along with what the writer wants.

Here's how it works:

Set the bit, using an example like this:

> *Do you want to go ahead and schedule a time tomorrow to close on the specifics of the proposal, or should we pencil in a day next week for a meeting?*

There's an element of confusion, or **misdirection** for the reader here. And typically, when readers are confused, they'll usually latch onto the first logical way out of that confusion. Focused, busy people will do whatever's necessary to keep out of the state of confusion.

When you use the word "or" in a bind, people will typically look for an opposite, more desirable path from the first option you're offering. And when they don't find one, they're often knocked off balance.

Here's how you put a bind in motion: While "talking" to your reader, lead with the bind. But don't stop after that—keep going.

Follow these steps:

1. Pinpoint the bind you want to lead with.
2. Make it a declarative sentence.
3. After you present the bind, keep talking (writing).
4. Pose a final, pointed question to nail it all down.

Like this approach, which pushes your reader to make a decision:

> *I'm positive that before the close of business today, you'll agree that the team's recommendations are the best way to go, or you'll review the benefits of the whitepaper one more time tonight and present your decision tomorrow. Either way, what counts is that you're giving the matter careful consideration, which benefits everybody. Wouldn't that be the best path forward?*

The bind serves to somewhat confuse the reader so they'll accept the first logical way out. And how convenient. The question at the end provides that way out (by re-focusing their attention to your desired outcome).

> **CAUTION:** *People resist change—even change in point of view—when they feel threatened. Avoid making your audience defensive by reframing threats to become opportunities for change. Set up a perceived* **win-win** *scenario for you and your "consumer."*

WHEN TO USE MANIPULATIVE LANGUAGE

Absolutely. The chief aim of business writing is to be understood. This means you're communicating with precision and clarity, using as few words as possible.

You wouldn't, for example, write *sporting event* when you're talking about a *football game*. Sporting event covers a lot more than just football; it's too general for your reader to get the right mental image you're shooting for when you're talking about a winning field goal in overtime.

It's true, most of the time the goal is to write clearly. But there are some business situations that require writers to be *purposely vague*. These would be the times when you have to achieve a strategic objective that's out of the ordinary, like:

- Putting a softer spin on a tough, unpleasant message
- Concealing the true meaning of a message, or even suggesting a different meaning altogether
- Remaining neutral on an issue because it's strategically favorable to your position.

Take a look at what I mean. Consider these two sentences:

Aragon Corporation issues guilty plea and agrees to pay $75 million in damages.

Aragon Corporation releases statement confirming $75 million settlement agreement.

They're both talking about the same event, right? But they're certainly doing it in different ways. The tone and slant of the first sentence is vastly different from the second. This is because each sentence reflects a unique agenda that's designed for different audiences.

Break it down. The first sentence could be a headline in *The Wall Street Journal,* while the second might be a general announcement on the home page of a company's website.

The second sentence puts a more positive spin on bad news by avoiding the negative term "guilty." This communication could be a message going out to stockholders, who, like all of us, associate a very definite, unfavorable meaning to the word "guilty." So each of these sentences is intended to manipulate the perception of a specific audience for a specific reason.

Want to know where you can find other examples? Read the message from the president of a company that had a lousy financial year. Or notice the language in that full-page newspaper ad from the CEO of the company that just got fined hundreds of millions of dollars for an oil spill that polluted the Gulf of Mexico.

Make no mistake. To purposely write in a vague style is a skill. Some might say not always an admirable one, but it's a skill that power writers can and should call upon when they need to.

Remember, your goal is primarily to **persuade**. And manipulative language goes to the *heart* of persuasion.

A QUICK WORD ABOUT SPIN DOCTORS AND SOUND BITES

While we're on the subject of manipulating language, understand that SPIN is an integral part of writing in the business world. You can't get away from it—so don't try to. Instead, look for ways to make it work for you. Spin is not necessarily a bad thing.

> **TO DO:** For some good, actionable input on how spin and other forms of manipulative language are used in business today, I recommend these two books:
>
> *The Language of Trust: Selling Ideas in a World of Skeptics*—Michael Maslansky, Prentice-Hall, 2011
>
> *The New Doublespeak: Why No One Knows What Anyone's Saying Anymore*—William Lutz, Harper Collins Publishers, 1996

GOOD NEWS/BAD NEWS

Conventional wisdom says that bad news should always start on a positive note in order to make the negative easier to hear. But if you start with a positive comment, you lessen the sincerity and the impact of the negative content that follows.

Here's the way to handle it:

Bring out the bad news first.

I read somewhere that people with ambition don't want to listen to a steady stream of positives, because negative news is what provides opportunities. That's why it's important to build emotional strength with your words by *offering up the bad news first*.

Offer positive comments next.

When the positive opinion comes after the negative one, it's perceived as an act of solidarity and generosity. (It also lessens the anger that the initial criticism may evoke.)

Require a follow-up.

"*We need to discuss this soon*" should be an important element of your end game. It suggests a deadline for action, and underscores the idea that you're setting the way for ongoing, goal-directed interactions.

Bad:

> *I look forward to hearing from you at your convenience.*
> *Perhaps we can meet some other time to discuss further.*
> *Just let me know.*
> *I'll stand by for your reply.*

Good:

> *I'll call next week to confirm a time to follow up with you.*
> *Let's talk again. When would be a good time?*
> *Can we talk again on the first of the month?*
> *What's a good time to get back to you?*

Always end with a "Thanks" or "Thank you." And the thank-you must not be automatic—it must be *felt*. You should always show gratitude toward the person on the other side of the transaction.

DRIVING RESULTS: THE GOOD NEWS/BAD NEWS LETTER

The good news/bad news letter is one of the best examples of immediate, *results-driven* writing you can produce. It's your clear, directed way ahead when you have a complaint you want resolved.

The letter has four basic components:

- A *positive opening*—one that sets the stage by laying out the problem
- The *bad news*
- A *proposed solution*
- A "peace pipe," or offering of *goodwill*.

Your **opening** should establish a tone of friendly rapport with your reader by bringing up something positive about your past experience with the company, individual, or product. This comes across as good news, and it sets the stage for mutual connection. It immediately brings the reader over to your side.

Then your **middle paragraph** delivers the bad news. Here, you're staying on-point, keeping clear and direct about the problem—as you see it. Be careful not to overdo it. Give only as much explanation as your reader needs. But don't go into anything your reader won't care about or doesn't need to know. Again, keep it short and focused.

Finally, your **closing paragraph** should propose a solution to the problem. What are you looking for? What do you want your reader to <u>do</u>? Do you want a refund, an exchange, or a credit to your account?

> **NOTE:** *When you offer a solution, you're saving your reader time. There won't be a need to call you to find out how you would like the problem settled.*

Be tactful and diplomatic. If you sound angry or abrasive, you won't motivate anybody to solve your problem quickly.

Here's an example of a good news/bad news letter (or email), written to the manager of a car rental business.

Dear Mr. Hammels:

I've always depended on A-Jax Car Rental for a quick, reliable response to my car rental needs. Without fail, you and the folks in your office have answered the call during many of my past business travel engagements. I've always been satisfied with the service I've received from A-Jax.

But your string of excellent service ended on July 11, 2001, when the car rental experience I had through your office turned out to be far less than satisfactory. Despite your assurance that you would have a car available, it turned out there was no car at all for me when I arrived at your office. So I was forced to threaten to call another rental company all the way across town to locate one. Only then were you able to find a rental for me. I missed an important meeting at work because of this, and I had to contact all parties involved to request a reschedule. Fortunately for me, they were OK with a new meeting date.

I'm sure you'll agree that it's unreasonable to charge me $199.00 for a compact car that was offered up well after my required time frame. So I would appreciate at least a partial refund on the Visa account you have on record for me.

Thank you for your consideration. Assuming we can reach a mutually agreeable solution to this most unfortunate incident, I look forward to calling on A-Jax for my car rental needs in the future.

Sincerely,

Bob Gardner

LIFE, DEATH, AND THE PSYCHOLOGY OF EMAIL

Make-or-break, situation-based writing. It's the heartbeat of business. Deals are made, careers are launched, connections are fostered, and expectations are managed—all via instant, warts-and-all, electronic messaging technology. **Email**.

Depending on how skilled we are at using it, email can be our best friend, or our worst enemy. This is because, by its nature, much of the email we write, reply to, and forward, is collaborative. It's not just limited to one recipient. It's broadcast to a global audience, to multiple readers. One-to-one, or one-to-many. Click and open. Add words and reply or forward. Done.

Email doesn't conform to the traditional rules. It leaves you, the writer, wide open for huge wins—or devastating failures.

The best (and, not coincidentally, the most successful) writers in business today are the ones who understand the unique characteristics and true potential of this vast, hyper-linked e-sandbox we're all playing in. And they're the ones who've discovered new and exciting ways to shape their writing to **capitalize** on it.

On top of it all, they're the writers with a crystal-clear lock on the value proposition that stands behind everything they produce. They're hungry for the opportunity to grow and prosper as effective communicators.

Here's some battle-tested tips for keeping your email under control...

Direct, immediate email subject lines get more results.

If you want your email to be read and acted on, you need a great subject line.

You only get one chance. Confuse your reader with a vague or sloppy headline and they won't elevate your message to the DO THIS NOW status it deserves. Slam-dunk, action subject lines take some practice, but you can do it.

Some examples:

Here's Our Most Serious Competitor
How We Can Benefit from The Magic of Dynamic Pricing
Look at this Great New Tool for Big Data Innovators
Take Two Minutes to Change Our Customer's World
The Time for Explosive Change at XYZ is Here. For Your Attention Now!

HOW TO DO EMAIL THE RIGHT WAY

Be concise, be simple, and **be direct**.

Never lose sight of who is reading the email and how you would talk with them **face to face**.

Provide a crystal-clear call to action and **include a deadline**.

The email that delivers results provides a straight, to-the-point intention or request that's linked to a specific timeframe for somebody to do something. Zero room for guesswork.

Prioritize. **Pick your spots**.

General George Patton once said "*Never fight a battle where nothing can be gained by winning.*" Is it really necessary to send that email? The more emails you send, the more others will have to do to prioritize your requests. By definition, then, you've lessened your chances of winning. If something can be better handled in person, do it. Save your ammunition for when it counts.

Avoid going back to the beginning of time.

Don't waste anybody's time by giving a long he-said, she-said commentary of events leading up to your point. It's always about *impact*. What happened, how this changes your reader's world, and what we need to do about it. (The same goes for PowerPoint slide decks, web site content, white papers, etc.)

Understand the characteristics of bad email.

Bad email is always too long, terribly written, has a boatload of attachments, and is hard to skim. We all know how to spot bad email.

Do not be a peddler of bad email.

Stock down: A sure-fire example of a cold call email that's DOA…

Dear Mr. Robinson:

Please allow me to introduce myself. My name is John Doe, Vice President of Business Development at SureFire Corporation. We are known as the premier business process optimization specialists for JobSoft in America. We get AP out of the paper chasing business and leverage your investment in JobSoft.

blah blah blah…

Seriously? Where's the focus on the reader's **pain point**?

Your odds of getting your reader to respond to a pitch like this are already 100 to 1 *against*.

Try something like this…

Dear Mr. Robinson:

Your business is unique in many ways, but I'm willing to bet you share at least one frustration with your competitors. You're probably spending too much time dealing with back office problems—like the problems that result from relying on an outdated, paper-based AP process.

I'm John Doe, Vice President of Business Development for JobSoft in America. We're here to help get you out of the paper-chasing business so you can get back to what you do best…

To bring this closer to home, think about what you have to lose by not staying aggressive with your writing approach.

Three things come to mind:

Reputation, Reputation, **Reputation**.

Marketing Guru Tom Peters calls it "Brand You."

> **CHECK OUT:** *"How to Communicate More Effectively in Email"* – by *Dave Johnson.*
>
> You can find it here: *http://www.cbsnews.com/8301-505143_162-28650375/how-to-communicate-more-effectively-in-email/*

GRAMMAR: THE ELEPHANT IN THE ROOM

RESPECT THE RULES—BUT DON'T *BOW* TO THEM

Alas, with writing, like so much else in life, there are rules. But we run into roadblocks when we confuse rules with restrictions. Grammar, spelling, punctuation, rhythm, focus, syntax, and structure aren't especially romantic terms, until you date them for awhile and get to know them better.

> **CONFESSION:** *I'm a linguistic rebel. "And" is one of my favorite ways to start a sentence, and if there's an infinitive around to ruthlessly split, I'm the guy with the sledge hammer and wedge.*

I'm also the last person you'll see parading around as some anal grammarian. To me, it's almost become a rule to break the rules. Sure, break the rules. But when you do, make it count. Because in a fast, short, and constantly evolving world, the assertive writers who make sense first, **win**.

> *"I love how the Internet has improved people's grammar far more than any English teacher has. If you write 'your' instead of 'you're' in English class all you get is a red mark. Mess up on the Internet, and may God have mercy on your soul."*
>
> —*Unknown (no doubt a victim)* —

NOT "CORRECTNESS"—*EFFECTIVENESS*

Today, it's not about correctness in writing; it's about effectiveness. The two don't necessarily have to go together. Many times they don't.

In sports, the only thing that counts is winning. Same with writing at work. You do what you have to do to score.

And for people who say they don't subscribe to "in your face" writing, I would say, get over it. Full Contact Writing requires you to get your point across rapidly. Its only aim is to move your reader to get behind your main point and run with it.

Yet, as we all know, taking risk is easier said than done. Sadly, many sharp, capable writers are afraid to break the rules of grammar and usage, afraid of being labeled incompetent. So they continue writing as they've always written. What happens? The finished product screams out self-conscious, self-doubt, *awkward.*

And some writers, relying on their smug self-assurance, are convinced they know the rules and fall back on their memory, or their college English handbooks, to nitpick the typos and small errors of their colleagues.

Most writers I've come in contact with fall somewhere in the middle. They're beleaguered by the do's and don'ts etched in their brains from their old grammar classes—so much so that they can no longer be assured, by their own cognizance, if they're writing well or not.

But in the world of Full Contact Writing, blind adherence to the rules is an irritant. Even higher than that, playing it "safe" is something that should be sprayed.

All of this calls for a new mindset. You have to know the rules to be able to break them (or at least bend them creatively and purposefully when you have to).

Great writing can't always be taught, but lousy writing is always preventable.

> "When comforting grammar nerds, hug them
> and whisper softly, *'there, they're, their.'"*
> —from *Grammarly.com*—

ESSENTIAL VS. "FAKE" RULES: KNOW THE DIFFERENCE!

While we're on the subject of grammar, you'll need to learn to distinguish between the essential, nonessential, and "fake" rules.

This is a must because ours is an age of abbreviated texts and tweets. We're in a time when the essentials of punctuation and usage tend to fall through the cracks.

FYI: *A recent Grammarly.com study of 100 LinkedIn profiles reported that in the same 10-year period, professionals who received from one to four promotions made 45% more grammatical errors than did professionals who were promoted six to nine times.*

Whether you're an entrepreneur, small business owner, manager, or an employee aspiring to any of these positions, you need to know how to write effectively. Of course, that means paying attention to grammar, spelling and punctuation, along with good word choice and a consistent style.

That's all well and good. But I say it's time for you to get beyond this expired, print-based focus on how writing "should" be developed and packaged.

Why bother moving outside the familiar? After all, as the old saying goes, *"If it doesn't pick my pocket or break my knee, why should I care?"* Well, you should care because most business writing falls short of that strong, sure-handed, *"this is why you should give me what I want"* impression you're after.

You should care because most people don't invest the time and effort it takes to succeed with their writing products like they do when they're watching over their investment portfolio.

Good writing means business. In the right hands, it's a powerful sales tool. It's an effective way to keep your target readership curious, engaged, and responsive.

Think of each piece of writing you create as the start of a conversation with a new customer. Why bore or alienate when you can entertain and **persuade**?

In many ways, business writing is *creative* writing.

WHEN TO IGNORE "PROPER ENGLISH" (AND WHEN NOT TO)

Abbreviations

Familiar abbreviations like "CD," "IT," and "DVD-R" are not only acceptable, they're preferable. It would sound stuffy, pretentious, if you spelled them out. On the other hand, online slang terms like "BTW" and "BRB" should be avoided except in texts or informal, conversational emails. And as for LOL, BFM, ROFL, and all that stuff—uh…**NOPE**.

Colloquialisms

Conventional wisdom holds that words like *"kids"* and *"guys,"* and sayings like *"nail Jell-O to the wall,"* should never be used in business writing. But if your document has a personal tone, and the terms are age-appropriate and not overly outdated and trite, they should be *good to go.*

Contractions

Used correctly, contractions like *"I'm," "won't,"* and *"they're"* have all but replaced full words, even in formal documents. **Use them.**

em Dashes

Once reserved for informal writing, these handy marks—expressing a thought within a thought—are now appropriate anywhere, in moderation.

Imperatives

As a rule, clarity is prized over old fashion courtesy in correspondence with people you know.

The jump ball:

> *We hope you'll remember to visit our booth at the trade show.*

The amplified version:

> *Remember to visit our booth at the trade show.*

A CRASH COURSE ON COMMAS

From my experience, the comma is the most frequently used—and abused—punctuation mark.

Rule of Thumb: Use commas to clarify or eliminate ambiguity.

Correct comma use:

- In series—to separate items:

    ...the wheel, the bridge, and the corps.

- To join independent clauses:

    Please submit our best and final offer by Monday, and I'll fax a copy to the head office.

- To set off essential material:

    Reid Blynn, the subcontractor's rep in the front row, was picked to be the point man.

That's all I want to say about commas. You can find everything else you ever wanted to know about comma usage on the wonderful worldwide Interweb. (Check the last section of this book for some sites you'll want to visit if you need more help.)

> *"My heroes are my parents,*
> *Superman and Wonder Woman."*
> *(*Use the extra comma. Keep it real.*)*
> —from *Grammerly.com*—

SECOND PERSON PRONOUNS (BRIEFLY)

Using "*one*" or "*the reader*" instead of "*you*"—as in "*One can hardly remember a time before cable television…*" has gone the way of the cassette tape.

BOTTLED SMOKE: THE GOOD, THE BAD, AND THE VERY UGLY

> *The requirement for initiative management and dynamic resource allocation arises from the need to better align strategic priorities with operational activities. The recommendation is that organizations engaging in CPM implementations consider introducing an initiative portfolio management function to affect alignment of resources and workforce activity prioritization with business priorities.*

This kind of writing is easy to recognize. It's full of impressive-sounding word combinations that convey no precise meaning. So, naturally, they're often seen as useful in business and military management, politics, and educational administration.

I have a theory about why these words are so pervasive. I believe it's because writers use vague word combinations to try to cover up imprecise thinking, or general lack of purpose. It's a smoke screen.

Now, some of these phrases have a longer shelf life than others. To be fair, they can be of some use. But as a writer you at least need to know what's still fresh and what's stale within your sphere of influence.

Current and topical buzzwords still have their place in your playbook, but don't overuse them. Plenty of writers still trot out these word "bluffs" in more than a few emails every day:

> *"interactive, empowerment, ownership, strategic, assessment, competency, validate, parameter, maximize, leverage, and paradigm."*

We can admit it. Most of us are guilty of sprinkling our writing with these cookie-cutter placeholders every now and then. It's too easy.

Besides, when you combine this nonspeak randomly you get some lofty-sounding (but still meaningless) phrases.

Like these:

> *analysis and validation of support strategies for customer satisfaction parameters*
>
> *maximized systems of strategic environmental processes*
>
> *parameters of team competency assessment support*
>
> *focus on ownership of teamwork assessment validation assets*
>
> *empowering your interactive competency team process*
>
> *utilizing paradigms of support validation strategies of assessment*

Isn't this a blast? You too can be management material!

I'm more than half serious here. Far too many people rely on this mix-and-match writing just to get by. For many, it's a crutch.

Now don't be upset with me because I'm not wearing the tennis shoes and waving the pom-poms here, but if you want more examples of this withering communication, just read your company's *"Mission Statement."*

To bring it all home, here's a big part of the problem. Many people down in the trenches sleepwalk their way through the writing part of their job. They're either numb to the process, or they're lazy—or both. More often than not, they simply lash words together under duress and a brutal deadline.

The result? Words go out that are dull, lifeless, incapable of evoking emotion, buy-in, or action. They're like birds trying to fly with dried mud under their wings. **EPIC FAIL**

You can avoid falling into this death spiral by thinking through all the relationships your words participate in, all the points where they touch people, and all the work they're asked to do.

ANATOMY OF A WINNING PARAGRAPH

The formula for bolting together a good paragraph never varies. Here's how it breaks down...

Opening: The topic sentence, the *key takeaway*.

The topic sentence tells your readers, point blank, exactly what you want them to know about a specific subject—and nothing else. It also helps guide your writing down the path to reader connection. That's exactly why a topic sentence is the *controlling idea* of a paragraph.

Sounds obvious, doesn't it? But you'd be amazed at how many writers overlook this point. They think they can simply keep writing until the main idea begins to somehow mysteriously define itself and the reader will just "get it."

Body: The mechanics of the "play" you're running; the extensions of your main idea that will help move the ball downfield.

The body holds the *supporting details* you assign to your topic sentence. Here's where you win or lose reader buy-in, so make sure all the parts are tying together—with no disconnects.

Methodical organization of detail is your one and only concern here.

Closing: The clincher that closes the loop.

The closing or clincher sentence comes after all the details have been carefully *layered* into the body of the paragraph. You've made your case and you're finishing it off with a final reminder about the central message. You're emphasizing its value, and how it relates to the reader's experience.

OK. That's a bare bones summary of the parts of a paragraph. Now take a look at how they fit together in the following ten-sentence example:

1. *Most companies fail.*
2. *In today's business world, that's almost a given.*
3. *It's an unsettling fact for young entrepreneurs, but old news to the seasoned veterans who've been tested in the world of start-ups.*
4. *But here's the good news: Experienced entrepreneurs know that running a company that eventually fails can actually help a career—but only if the executives are willing to view failure as a potential for improvement.*
5. *The statistics are disheartening no matter how an entrepreneur defines failure.*
6. *If "failure" means liquidating all assets, with investors losing most or all the money they put into the company, then the failure rate for start-ups is 30-40%, according to Shikhar Ghosh, a senior lecturer at Harvard Business School who has held top executive positions at some eight technology-based start-ups.*

7. *If "failure" refers to neglecting the projected return on investment, then the failure rate is 70-80%.*

8. *And if "failure" is defined as declaring a projection and then falling short of meeting it, then the failure rate is an astounding 90-95%.*

9. *By all accounts, few companies achieve their initial projections, say the experts.*

10. *Failure is not only expected. It's the norm.*

Here we start with an assertion as the **controlling idea** (sentence 1). From there, every sentence in the body of the paragraph (sentences 2-9) is dedicated to **amplifying the validity of the main topic** in the reader's mind.

Each one of the details provided in the paragraph body moves the ball downfield toward the goal line. By the time we get to the clincher (sentence #10) we've taken readers full circle and "**re-reminded**" them of the key point we registered in the first sentence.

The Main Point: Paragraphs aren't simply blocks of text. They must develop and convey a single, logical thought. So, if a paragraph seems to contain more than a single idea, break it up. Long blocks of text scare away readers like a firecracker spooks a house pet.

Oh, and another thing: When you're writing for online readers, *white space is your faithful friend.*

POWERPOINT: SOME FUNDAMENTAL TRUTHS

A NOTE FROM THE FIELD

Soldier's Diary: The Importance of PowerPoint Slides in Iraq

By Capt. Dan Sukman

BAGHDAD—Editor's note: At the time of this writing, U.S. Army Capt. Dan Sukman was serving a one-year deployment to Iraq.

May 3, 2006

"Approximately three days ago, I put together a PowerPoint briefing for my commander. It had the right info, but was not displayed in the proper manner. It's a lesson I have learned on this staff, and over the last six years in general: How you present information is often just as important as the information you present. When it comes to this job, if your audience, be it your boss or soldiers under you, doesn't understand the information you are trying to send across, they might make a decision based on the information they thought they heard, and it can cost lives.

As a staff officer, I have done a ton of briefings over here, some as short as 30 seconds, some a little longer. The amount of man hours put into briefings in Iraq, be it preparing scripts or getting graphics on a PowerPoint slide just right, must be astronomical. Don't even get me going on the number of slides printed out on these briefs. One running joke we have is $87 billion approved from Congress, $86 billion on paper and printer toner.

The true testament to the professionalism of soldiers out here is the briefings that occur every day at the squad level. Soldiers going out on patrol day in and day out get mission briefs from their squad leaders, platoon sergeants and platoon leaders for every mission. No fancy PowerPoint slides in these briefs, and they are usually conducted in a tent or adjacent to a HMMWV rather than a comfortable conference room.

Where it all ties together is the squad leader depends on accurate info from his platoon leader, who depends on accurate info from the company, which depends on accurate info from the battalion and brigade, where the decision for the operation was made. At any level, ***if information is not presented in an understandable, actionable manner, lives could be at stake****.*

It sounds like I am making a big deal about the mundane, the ability to brief affecting the lives of soldiers at the lowest level, but I will end this by paraphrasing my boss, who often states that when we look at a map ***"the pins on the map are not just pins, they are actual soldiers, and they are our soldiers."***

Understandable and actionable—the keys to every piece of writing you do.

SIX MORE MUST-KNOWS FOR POWERPOINT SUCCESS

- If it takes you more than 20 seconds to go over the contents of a slide, there are too many words.

- Never use full sentences in PowerPoint bullets. Always use the **shortest fragments** you can, and talk around them.

- Bullet points should be short and each should lead with an **action verb**.

- Maintain **parallel construction**. This creates a sense of rhythm within a sentence or paragraph, between paragraphs, or in a bulleted list.

- Don't get fancy with the cutesy backgrounds. They're distracting and annoying. Use black letters on a subdued background.

- Don't let your audience see you as "in the way" of their being able to read and absorb your slide messages. Use clear, engaging pictures and action verb-based phrases to tell your story.

The late Steve Jobs was a master at the art of PowerPoint presentations. If your tendency is to litter your slides with endless bullet points, complex graphics, and lots of "stuff," it would be time well spent for you to have a look at what Jobs could do with a slide presentation.

ANOTHER TIP: For some good, solid advice on doing PowerPoint the right way, check out:

Presentation Zen: Simple Ideas on Presentation Design and Delivery, Garr Reynolds, New Riders, 2011.

BUSINESS LETTERS DEMYSTIFIED

HOW TO WRITE ONE

"A good business letter can get you a job interview. Get you off the hook. Or get you money. It's totally asinine to blow your chances of getting WHATEVER you want—with a business letter that turns people off instead of turning them on."

—Malcolm Forbes
Former President and Editor-in-Chief
Forbes Magazine

Back in my undergraduate days I came across an ad in *Rolling Stone* magazine, placed there by the International Paper Company. At the time, the company was sponsoring a series of advertisements called "*Power of the Printed Word*," and this ad just clicked with me, so I photocopied it and put it in my notebook. (See, I *told* you I collect this stuff!)

This segment was a quick, two-page reprint offering some thoughts from Malcolm Forbes, on "*How to write a business letter*."

To this day, I haven't come across a better, more brass tacks overview on the subject. The ad starts with Forbes looking you right in the eye. He's coming at you as a guy who's talking from experience, and you'd better be paying attention. Here's somebody who knows what works in a business letter –and what doesn't. Not surprisingly, his rules still hold up today.

What follows is a summary of the approach Forbes believes separates the winners from the losers (most of it's just good common sense)—and (get this) it starts BEFORE you write your letter.

KNOW WHAT YOU WANT

If you don't, write it down—in one sentence. "*I want to get an interview within the next two weeks*." That simple. List the major points you want to get across. It'll keep you on course.

PLUNGE RIGHT IN

Call your recipient by name. NOT *"Dear Sir, Madam,* or *Ms."* *Dear Mr. Christanthopoulos*—and be sure to spell it right. Tell what your letter is about in the first paragraph. If you're answering a letter, refer to the date it was written, so your reader won't waste time hunting for it. Reading a letter shouldn't be a chore.

Reward your readers for the time they give you.

WRITE SO THEY'LL ENJOY IT

Write the entire communication from your reader's point of view. What's in it for them? Beat them to the draw. Surprise them by answering the questions and objections they might have. Be positive. Readers will be more receptive to what you have to say. Be natural. *Write the way you talk.*

The acid test—read your letter out loud when you're done. You might get a shock, but you'll know for sure if it sounds natural. Don't be cute or flippant. Have a sense of humor. Be specific.

Now you've got something to sink your teeth into.

Lean heavier on nouns and verbs, lighter on adjectives. Use the active voice instead of the passive. *Your writing will have more guts.*

GIVE IT THE BEST YOU'VE GOT

Make your message *appetizing*. Keep your letter short. Keep your paragraphs short. For emphasis, underline (or bold) important words. Make it perfect. Be crystal clear. Use good English. Don't put on airs.

EDIT RUTHLESSLY

SUM IT UP AND GET OUT

The last paragraph should tell the reader exactly what you want him to do—or what you're going to do. Short and sweet.

"Good luck," he says when he's done. "I hope you get what you're after."

Beautiful.

A DUMB LETTER

Here's an example of what *not* to do. Look at these opening paragraphs of a letter from a city department of licenses and inspections to new business owners:

> *INFORMATION SHEET FOR BUSINESSES*
>
> *In order to conduct business in our city, you are required to complete an application for a Business Tax Account Number and a Business Privilege license. The license fee is $200.00 and is a one-time charge.*
>
> *The establishment of a Business Tax account number would subject you to our city's Business tax ordinances and regulations as follows:*
>
> *BUSINESS PRIVILEGE TAX-Levied on annual gross receipts and net income which is attributable to the taxpayer's privilege of doing business in our city at the following rates...*

Now, if I were a small business owner looking to bring my company to this city, I would have definite reactions to receiving a letter like this. I wouldn't mind so much paying a city business privilege tax. What I *would* mind, a great deal, would be the tone of the letter. The stop-watch, bench-press mentality reflected in this ultimatum is not only cold, it borders on being downright nasty.

- No salutation.

- No warm welcome to the city's business community. (And the city damn well <u>should</u> welcome me; I hope to be paying it a lot of tax money in the coming years.)

- No wishing me luck in my new venture.

It's Full Contact Writing gone wrong. That's unfortunate, because a product like this is the one element that still makes the business letter stand apart from all other media.

Here's a better way…

Dear _____:

Welcome to the <city name> business community. We wish you all the best for future success.

To get you started on the right track as a new business owner in <city name>, we're providing the following essential licensing information:

INFORMATION SHEET FOR NEW BUSINESSES

In order to conduct business in <city name>, you'll need to complete an application for a Business Tax Account Number and a Business Privilege license. The one-time charge for this license fee is $200.00.

Once you've obtained your license and a Business Tax account number, you'll need to be aware of the following Business tax ordinances and regulations:

BUSINESS PRIVILEGE TAX-Levied on annual gross receipts and net income which is attributable to the taxpayer's privilege of doing business in our city at the following rates...

Please contact us if you have any questions. We're happy to assist you in making the process as smooth as possible.

Again, welcome!

Remember, a letter like this is a highly personal, one-to-one communication that can do one of three things:

Establish and strengthen a relationship
Do nothing—have no effect
Be negative and destructive.

JOB SEEKERS: NAIL THE COVER LETTER!

Sure, there are hundreds of books on how to write a resume. We all tend to key on the resume as our primary self-promotion tool when we're on the hunt for a new job. And rightly so.

But don't overlook the power and potential of the cover letter in your search! It's the first thing your reader's going to see, and its only job is to get them to move on to what follows—your resume. So the cover letter is an important marketing tool in its own right.

I've used the following cover letter format many times and it gets *good* results. In fact, I've had recruiters *thank me* for sending them this type of letter with my resume. They told me I made their job easier, and saved them a lot of time by showcasing the information they needed to see, right away.

I call it the "T" cover letter, because the body of the letter consists of a simple, two-column table. Each side of the "T" provides a bulleted list. The left side of the table lines up the company's top-level job requirements (as specified in their announced opening) with specific elements of my background and experience on the right side.

> **NOTE:** If your background and qualifications don't match up <u>exactly</u> with the job requirements, but you have skills that relate, or might translate, to what the employer's looking for, change the "*My Background and Experience*" column to "*My Related Background and Experience.*"

With the "T" letter as the body of your email, and your resume attached, a prospective employer can get a quick picture of how and why your credentials deserve a closer look.

BOTTOM LINE: Cover letters (emails) don't have to be complicated. I know this simple, direct approach works, because employers told me that it was the key factor that led to their decision to call me.

The basic "T" letter format looks like this:

Dear *[recipient]*:

I'm applying for the position of <*specific job title*>, as advertised recently in/on <*name of source location*>. Please review my attached resume against your current or projected needs.

As the following summary table clearly shows, there's a seamless match between your position requirements and my background and experience.

[INSERT THE 2-COLUMN TABLE HERE]

This is a great opportunity for me to make an immediate contribution to XYZ's ongoing business success, and I would be happy to meet with you, at your earliest convenience, to further discuss the many positives I will bring to your organization in the role of <*position title*>.

I look forward to following up with you in the near future.

Sincerely,

RG Gardner

EMULATE SUCCESS

The best writing rules can't always be stated, but you can learn them by reading good, solid writing—every kind of writing. Start attuning your eye (and ear) to all sorts of writing styles geared to a variety of situations.

> *"If you want to be successful, find someone who has achieved the results you want and copy what they do and you'll achieve the same results."*
> —Tony Robbins—

Good examples of high-fiber words at work can be found everywhere.

And again, don't discount the potential value of that junk mail that creeps into your mailbox. You never know what you can discover in this unsolicited marketing material. Why do you think this writing made its way to your kitchen table? Because it's been proven to persuade. Try to figure out why. Study it. Make what you learn part of your best practices as a power writer.

> **TIP:** I use a software program that lets me keep all my notes in a handy index form. The simple to use program makes content retrieval fast and easy. It's called *Personal Knowbase*. You can find out more about this productivity application by going to *www.bitsmithsoft.com*.

A high-charged word combination here, a quick-burst sentence there. It's all grist for your mill. Look for writing that hooks you. If you know what works in a given scenario—what *sounds* good—you'll start to copy it.

THE BEAT GOES ON: "BORROW" WHAT WORKS

"All my best thoughts were stolen by the ancients."
—*Ralph Waldo Emerson*—

Word hoarding. It's a reflection of the current Western postmodern lifestyle—fashion, music, art, architecture, industrial and graphic design—and it's characterized by: **Reuse**.

We live in the cut and paste era. Accept it and make it work for you.

"You go for the points of maximum anxiety," one copywriter says. "You figure out what keeps people up at 4 in the morning and then promise salvation, or at least the hope of salvation. Collecting the best samples of persuasive writing is a good habit to get into. **Smart Stealing** definitely makes sense as a writing strategy."

If good words come from something you've heard on the radio, or TV commercial, or an ad in the newspaper, or a magazine sound bite, use them. Add them to your tool box.

You want to harness the life, the sound, and the strength of the dialogue, the words that are flowing around you, and make it all part of your communication process.

But don't forget this important fact:

Words are everywhere. Good ones aren't.

FOUR TAKEAWAYS FROM ERNEST HEMINGWAY

Many people faced with the task of writing for the world of work are quick to throw up their hands and admit defeat before they start. "What do you want from me?" they'll moan, "I'm no Hemingway."

But if you want to learn the basics of "cut-to-the-chase" writing, there's no better master than Hemingway. His writing style is the model for simplicity and clarity. And he can offer us some great advice for making our business writing more effective—like these four tips:

1. Use **short sentences**.

Hemingway was famous for a sparse, no fluff style of writing that moved right to the point. Some say he wrote with "simple genius." When he was challenged with a $10 bet to write an entire story in no more than six words, he came up with this:

"For sale: baby shoes, never worn."

2. Use **short first paragraphs** (a logical extension of tip #1).

3. Use **vigorous English**.

He's talking about English that's forceful, muscular, *vigorous*. Writing that springs from passion, focus, and intention. It's the difference between putting in a "good try" and *getting the job done*.

4. **Be positive**, not negative.

Writers should say what something *is* rather than what it isn't. This means you're using "up" words instead of language that's negative. Negativity in your writing steers your readers in a direction that runs counter to where you want to take them. To call a task "effortless," for example, still puts your reader's focus on the word "effort." *Accentuate the positive.*

Change:

"inexpensive" to economical
"painless" to comfortable
"error-free" to consistent
"foolproof" to stable

For my money, Hemingway was one of the charter members of the school of **FULL CONTACT WRITING**.

10 FINAL HINTS ON HOW TO WRITE

Some of the tightest, most effective writing comes from the world of advertising. Here's some priceless and uncompromising advice from a different kind of cultural icon: legendary businessman (and some say the original *Mad Man*) David Ogilvy. (Note: A few points are a bit outdated, but there's still plenty of timeless wisdom here.)

On September 7th, 1982, Ogilvy sent the following internal memo to all agency employees, titling it "*How to Write*."

"The better you write, the higher you go in Ogilvy & Mather," he said. "People who think well, write well. Good writing is not a natural gift. You have to learn to write well..."

Then he went on to offer his people these 10 hints:

1. Read the Roman-Raphelson book on writing. Read it three times. (*Writing That Works, 3e: How to Communicate Effectively in Business* [Kenneth Roman, Joel Raphelson])
2. Write the way you talk. Naturally.
3. Use short words, short sentences, and short paragraphs.
4. Never use jargon words like *reconceptualize, demassification, attitudinally, judgmentally*. They are hallmarks of a pretentious ass.
5. Never write more than two pages on any subject.
6. Check your quotations.
7. Never send a letter or a memo on the day you write it. Read it aloud the next morning—and then edit it.
8. If it is something important, get a colleague to improve it.
9. Before you send your letter or memo, make sure it is crystal clear what you want the recipient to do.
10. If you want IMMEDIATE ACTION, don't write. Go and tell the guy what you want.

FOR GOOD MEASURE: MORE TOOLS FOR WRITERS

> *"Intelligence is not the ability to store information, but to know where to find it."*
> —Albert Einstein—

Check out these books for everything you ever needed or wanted to know about grammar, punctuation, and all things *wordage*. These are some of the most informative, interesting, and recommended books on grammar you'll find out there today. You can pick up most of these books at better bookstores. All are available on *Amazon.com*.

- *The Elements of Expression: Putting Thoughts into Words*—Arthur Plotnik

- *Eats, Shoots & Leaves: The Zero Tolerance Approach to Punctuation* — Lynne Truss

- *The Elements of Style, Fourth Edition* — William Strunk Jr., E. B. White, and Roger Angell (Foreword)

- *The Deluxe Transitive Vampire: The Ultimate Handbook of Grammar for the Innocent, the Eager, and the Doomed* — Karen Elizabeth Gordon

- *Garner's Modern American Usage* — Bryan A. Garner

- *The Great Typo Hunt: Two Friends Changing the World, One Correction at a Time* — Jeff Deck, Benjamin D. Herson

- *Things That Make Us (Sic): The Society for the Promotion of Good Grammar Takes on Madison Avenue, Hollywood, the White House, and the World* — Martha Brockenbrough

- *Woe Is I: The Grammarphobe's Guide to Better English in Plain English* — Patricia T. O'Conner

- *The Elements of Grammar*—Margaret Shertzer

- *Forgotten English* — Jeffrey Kacirk

- *The Chicago Manual of Style* — University of Chicago Press Staff
- *The Associated Press Stylebook and Briefing on Media Law 2011* — Associated Press
- *The Only Grammar Book You'll Ever Need: A One-Stop Source for Every Writing Assignment* — Susan Thurman
- *You Are What You Speak: Grammar Grouches, Language Laws, and the Politics of Identity* — Robert Lane Greene
- *Better Punctuation in 30 Minutes a Day* — Ceil Cleveland
- *The Language of Trust: Selling Ideas in a World of Skeptics* — Michael Maslansky
- *The New Doublespeak: Why No One Knows What Anyone's Saying Anymore* —William Lutz

A FEW GOOD BLOGS ON BUSINESS WRITING

www.businesswritingblog.com
http://blogs.hbr.org/2013/07/your-company-is-only-as-good-a/
http://blog.intuit.com/marketing/10-sins-of-business-writing/

SOME GREAT WEBSITES FOR HELP WITH GRAMMAR

www.dictionary.com
www.thesaurus.com
www.lousywriter.com
www.dailygrammar.com
www.dailywritingtips.com
www.writing.com
www.grammarly.com

MORE WEBSITES ON WORDS
(AND HOW BEST TO USE THEM)

https://owl.english.purdue.edu/owl/resource/
http://grammar.ccc.commnet.edu/grammar/concise.htm
http://grammar.about.com/
http://www.bartleby.com/strunk/
http://www.writerswrite.com/businesscommunications/
http://www.plain-text.co.uk

FOR YOUR ROAD AHEAD

FIVE REMINDERS

- Never back off from trying innovative ways to express yourself – with writing that works <u>for</u> you, not *against* you.

- Never overlook or compromise the potential Return on Investment (ROI) of your words in your haste to make a deadline.

- Always assume that most of the time your readers don't want to give you anything, not even an opportunity. If that doesn't keep you focused on finding a writing edge, *nothing* will.

- Stay on the hunt for high-torque, high-impact words that can and do get people to act. (Here's a website you should visit: *Power Words for Emotional Selling*: http://www.freereports.net/powerwords.html)

- Steal ideas from the media writers and bloggers. That's right. I said "steal" (not verbatim, or course). It's the voice of the world. Journalists and bloggers are skilled at getting to the point quickly and with memorable, yet simple words and analogies.

And finally…

Practice, Perfect, WIN!

ABOUT THE AUTHOR

R.G. (Bob) Gardner is a management consultant, business communication strategist, and devoted practitioner of **Full Contact Writing**. His background features a strong combination of formal education in linguistics, rhetoric, and the language arts—coupled with deep, corporate experience in technical writing, marketing communications, and proposal development.

Bob's impressive list of writing wins stems from successful advisory staff and management positions with such world-leading technology corporations as RCA, General Electric, Lockheed Martin, and Computer Sciences Corporation.

His eclectic, ever-expanding body of work includes books, articles, columns, reviews, essays, and an impressive showcase of winning proposals and dynamic web content. Bob's content has appeared in *Small Press Review, Technical Communication,* Bowling Green University *Interchange, Martinsburg Journal, Atlantic Publishing, Philadelphia Inquirer, Critical Inquiry, Rio Grande Currents*, and on a broad, growing number of websites across a wide range of industries and market segments.

A recognized authority in writing, editing, and corporate communication strategy, Gardner holds a BA in Political Science and Economics, an MA in English, an MS in Technical and Professional Communication, and a doctorate in the Language Arts.

Bob is founder and managing partner of *The GardComm Group*, a management consulting firm specializing in business communication services and solutions, proposal support, and brand promotion for corporations and start-ups alike.

Contact Bob via email at: *gardcommgroup@gmail.com*

INDEX

"T" LETTER FORMAT, 106
ABBREVIATIONS, 91
ABRAHAM LINCOLN, 22
ACE, 12, 13, 61, 62
ACTION LANGUAGE, 6
AGE OF IMMEDIACY, 4
ALBERT EINSTEIN, 111
ANALOGY, 54
AUDIENCE, 10, 11, 12, 14, 15, 17, 18, 19, 20, 21, 24, 26, 27, 28, 30, 40, 41, 44, 56, 67, 77, 79, 81, 85, 98, 99
BEHAVIOR CHANGE, 35
BINDS, 78
BLOGS, 1, 74
BOB DYLAN, 7
BUSINESS LETTER, 101, 104
BUZZWORDS, 44, 94
CAPTAIN BARBOSSA, 72
CHANGINGMINDS.ORG, 77
CICERO, 14
COLLOQUIALISMS, 92
COMMA, 72, 92, 93
COMMAS, 92, 93
CONTRACTIONS, 92
COVER LETTER, 105
CULTURE OF ATTENTION, 66
CURT SCHILLING, 68
DAN SUKMAN, 98
DAVE JOHNSON, 88
DAVID OGILVY, 110
DESCRIPTIVE NOUNS, 41
DIRECT ADDRESS, 56
DIRECTIONAL CUES, 48
EM DASHES, 92
EMAIL, 47, 63, 64, 66, 71, 75, 76, 77, 84, 85, 86, 87, 88, 105, 115
ERIC SCHMIDT, 1
ERNEST HEMINGWAY, 76
FORCING FUNCTION, 68
FRAGMENTS, 8, 11, 52, 99
FULL CONTACT WRITING, 4, 5, 6, 9, 10, 11, 26, 36, 59, 60, 62, 74, 89, 90, 104, 109, 115
GARR REYNOLDS, 100
GEORGE ORWELL, 49
GOOD NEWS/BAD NEWS, 81, 83, 84
GRABBY WRITING, 75
GRAMMARLY.COM, 90, 91
HYPE, 29
IMAGERY, 54
IMPERATIVES, 92
INFINITIVE LEAD, 57
JAKOB NIELSEN, 14
JARGON, 37, 39, 40, 44, 110
JEFF BEZOS, 63
JOHN LENNON, 42, 62
KILLER PARAGRAPHS, 53
LAYERED TARGET SEGMENT, 18
LINE OF SIGHT, 17
LOU GERSTNER, 28
LOUIS C.K., 58
LOUIS PASTEUR, 21
MALCOLM FORBES, 101
MARK TWAIN, 3
MARSHALL MCLUHAN, 70
METAPHOR, 54, 55, 56
MICHAEL MASLANSKY, 81, 112
NIKE, 77
OPENING, 34, 51, 53, 57, 83, 103, 105
PARAGRAPH, 46, 51, 53, 61, 73, 95, 96, 97, 99, 102
PARALLEL CONSTRUCTION, 99
PAUL GOODMAN, 43
PERSONAL KNOWBASE, 107
POINTED VERBS, 41
POWER WORDS, 29, 41

PowerPoint, 45, 86, 98, 99, 100
primary target, 17
questions, 53
Ralph Waldo Emerson, 108
return on investment (ROI), 114
Robin Williams, 43
Roy H. Williams, 6
Rumsfeld method, 49, 54
Scott Berkun, 68
secondary audience, 17, 18, 20
sentence, 8, 23, 24, 33, 34, 37, 41, 43, 46, 50, 52, 53, 56, 57, 58, 61, 72, 73, 79, 80, 89, 95, 96, 97, 99, 101, 107
slang, 44, 92
smart stealing, 108
speech acts, 3
spin, 80, 81
Stafford Green, 33
Stanley Kubrick, 23

Stephen King, 42, 76
Steve Jobs, 24, 100
Strunk and White, 21
Sun Tzu, 12
The Elements of Style, 21, 61, 111
the question, 58, 73
thesaurus.com, 40
Tim Radford, 45
Tom Peters, 9, 88
Tom Stoppard, 37
Tony Robbins, 107
transition words, 50
WIIFM, 19
Wilbert E. Moore, 75
William Lutz, 81, 112
William Strunk Jr., 61, 111
WIN system, 13, 61
word management, 37
www.bitsmithsoft.com, 107

www.ingramcontent.com/pod-product-compliance
Lightning Source LLC
Chambersburg PA
CBHW051720170526
45167CB00002B/736